FAMILY

How to have
a healthy
Christian home

Compiled and Edited by
Hal Donaldson, Ken Horn,
Ann Floyd & Joel Kilpatrick

Pentec(
Published by

D1041631

Dedicated to Billie Davis for her contribution to Christian families around the world.

Special recognition to the staff of the *Pentecostal Evangel*: Barbara Chapman, Randy Clute, Jodi Harmon, Rebekah Haught, Ron Kopczick, John Maempa, Kirk Noonan, Ashli O'Connell and Sarah Simmons.

Cover design by Randy Clute

Library of Congress Catalog Card Number 99-67931
International Standard Book Number 0-88243-342-3
Printed in the United States of America

Introduction

There has perhaps never been a time when the family has been under such severe attack from the enemy. I don't need to remind you of the divorce statistics or the heartache when people go through this tragedy. It's very possible that many of you have a family member who has experienced a divorce.

Why is the family going through such disarray? Because God loves the family; and anything God loves, the enemy hates.

Outside of the church of Jesus Christ, the family is the greatest institution on earth. God created marriage to be a unique, wonderful arrangement to serve as a model of the way He loves His people and unites with them. It is a special relationship between male and female that is to be preserved with great effort and unrelenting stamina.

In this important book, the authors have touched on the critical needs of the family. Experts have written on how to ensure that your marriage and family will not just exist, but enjoy health, grow in love and become stronger as the years pass. Whatever your situation, God wants to help you succeed in your marriage. As you read *How To Have a Healthy Christian Home,* ask God to speak to you about your family and how you can be an example of His love to a world that has lost hope.

— Wayde I. Goodall, chairman
Marriage and Family Committee
Assemblies of God

Contents

Foreword

The family is God's invention. He made us to be fulfilled in relationships.

This book has principles to help you build a home that honors God. Here are four steps to consider as you read this book:

1. Make people more important than things.

As husband and wife, take whatever steps are necessary to make your relationship with Christ what you want it to be. Be sure you take good care of each other. No family is stronger than the marriage on which it is built.

Then ask, "What can we do so our children will have the greatest opportunity to become healthy adults?"

The common denominator I see in family histories of hurting people is the pain rooted in a damaged or broken home life. When you give your children a healthy marriage to observe and extend to them appropriate love and discipline, you provide for them a quality of life money cannot buy.

2. Spend time with the people who count in your life.

At least once every several weeks, take two or three hours alone with your mate doing something both of you enjoy.

Be sure your children will have pleasant memories of their growing-up years. Do something at least once a week that they enjoy. When they become teen-agers, they will spend more time with their friends, but they will still enjoy family get-togethers.

If possible, keep your children in the care of a parent or grandparent until they are 3 years of age. If the wife has a career, her husband will need to be more involved with parenting.

Share time with other couples, but don't let them invade your private time.

3. Provide healthy love and discipline for each child.

When your children are small, give them plenty of physical affection. As they grow older, verbalize your love daily. No one should ever go to sleep in your home without knowing he or she is loved.

Frequent manifestations of love equip a child to benefit from healthy discipline. Don't discipline each child alike. Each is different in disposition and will need to be trained in "the way he should go" (Proverbs 22:6, NIV).

Read books about parenting.

4. Stay in close relationship with the Lord.

For your children, you are what it means to be Christians. Build religious traditions into their memories. See that thanks is expressed at every meal. Let your children see you sing, pray and worship together.

My prayer is that God will use this book to help you make good family decisions, because your family is your fortune.

RICHARD D. DOBBINS, PH.D.

MARRIAGE

"Marriage should be honored by all."

— Hebrews 13:4 (NIV)

1

MARRIAGE ON GOD'S TERMS

By Edgar Lee

A nice-looking young couple visited the church I served. Both had been reared in churches in another city and had pursued careers to our metropolis. I discovered they were living together without benefit of marriage.

Like almost 2 million couples today, they had accepted the reasoning expressed in a popular song that forgotten words and dried ink stains from marriage ceremonies and licenses do not matter.

In such a world, believers must turn to the Bible to find what marriage is and what is required to make it succeed.

Biblical Foundations

Marriage was created by God to be a permanent, faithful union between one man and one woman. Whatever the ceremony, marriage is sacred and vital to our nature as human beings made in the image of God.

God showed us that He carefully and deliberately "created man in his own image . . . male and female he created them" (Genesis 1:27*). The purpose of the two sexes is clear in Genesis 2 where God banished the loneliness and incompleteness of Adam by taking a part of his side, usually trans-

*All Scripture references in this chapter are from the New International Version.

lated "rib," and created Eve to be his wife.

God himself brings man and woman together and institutes marriage for all time. "For this reason a man will leave his father and mother and be united to his wife, and they will become one flesh" (Genesis 2:24). Throughout the Bible this commandment is foundational to understanding marriage. Jesus repeated it in His teaching in Matthew 19:4-6 and Mark 10:6-9. Paul repeated it in Ephesians 5:31.

God ordered three vital steps to be taken to enter into marriage:

1. *Partners must leave father and mother.* God dictated emotional and physical distance to bring about a new family unit.

2. *The man and woman are to be united.* Both the King James Version and the New American Standard Version translate the Hebrew term, which has the idea of "clinging" or "sticking to," with the more powerful but archaic word "cleave." God commanded couples to cling tightly together, as though glued, through the challenges and changes of life. The bond is powerful and permanent.

Jesus emphasized: "What God has joined together, let man not separate" (Matthew 19:6). The Greek word for "joined" means "to yoke together," as the ancient farmer would lay a double yoke over the necks of two oxen. In marriage God does the yoking. No person can abandon the union without consequences.

3. *Couples are to become one flesh.* Marriage must be consummated sexually; and regular sexual union, as Paul noted (1 Corinthians 7:3-5), must take place to fulfill the Creator's intention and to experience the tender, intimate, mystical bonding of husband and wife. So precious is this sexual union that Paul shuddered to think one should join in a "one-flesh" union with another sexual partner (1 Corinthians 6:16).

In Genesis is the understanding that marriage is a covenant. Steeped in human equality, we have come to think of it as a legal contract between equal partners subject to a no-fault dissolution under certain conditions. The marriage covenant, by contrast, is effected in relationship with God.

He creates. He pairs. He bonds. He dictates permanence.

When divorce threatened the stability of society, God thundered through His prophet, "I hate divorce" (Malachi 2:16). He reminded His people of their marriage covenant with each other and with Him. "The Lord is acting as the witness between you and the wife of your youth, because you have broken faith with her, though she is your partner, the wife of your marriage covenant. Has not the Lord made them one? In flesh and spirit they are his" (Malachi 2:14,15).

Dynamic Relationship

God intends marriage to be a growing, changing, enriching intimacy until finally transcended in a resurrected and angel-like perfection in His eternal presence. (See Matthew 22:30.) This idea can only be accomplished by hard work and perseverance that take advantage of resources our Heavenly Father provides.

His Word challenges the natural sinfulness and selfishness of each partner and describes the proper conduct.

The Word commands that believers "not be yoked together with unbelievers" (2 Corinthians 6:14). While marriage to an unbeliever is valid and binding under God, it is out of harmony with His will and lacks the shared experiences of His Word and Spirit.

By divine order married Christians are caught in a love triangle. God is at the apex watching over the rights and responsibilities of each partner who is joined at the base to the other and to Him in a mutually accountable relationship.

Paul defined this relationship of partners under God. Before God, each partner has equal standing. "There is neither . . . male nor female . . . you are all one in Christ Jesus" (Galatians 3:28). Spirit-filled husbands and wives "submit to one another out of reverence for Christ" (Ephesians 5:21). Adam remembered that Eve came from his side to be a beloved partner, not to be a mindless servant.

"Husbands, love your wives, just as Christ loved the church and gave himself up for her" (Ephesians 5:25). The

Greek verb is *agapao,* signifying the highest, self-giving form of love—a love that is not dependent upon feelings. Husbands are to "love their wives as their own bodies. He who loves his wife loves himself" (Ephesians 5:28). As Christ died for the Church, Christian husbands are willing to support their wives, not just financially, but in all aspects of marriage.

In that setting Paul's command to set the husband as head of the family is not oppressive but is necessary for an orderly society. "Wives, submit to your husbands as to the Lord" (Ephesians 5:22).

Selfless commitment to the marriage covenant requires a love energized by the Holy Spirit. Paul prefaced his teaching on marriage with the command, "Be filled with the Spirit" (Ephesians 5:18). He does so because the Spirit communicates love. "God has poured out his love [*agape*] into our hearts by the Holy Spirit, whom he has given us" (Romans 5:5).

Fellowship

God supports His institutions of marriage and family with a community of believers, the Church, headed by Christ, guided by His Word and vitalized by His Spirit. The family is a little church in need of a bigger church which must take seriously the command, "Let us not give up meeting together . . . but let us encourage one another" (Hebrews 10:25).

The word "encourage" translates from the Greek *parakaleo* which meant literally "to call alongside" and more generally "to exhort" or "to comfort." Encouraging or exhorting is a gift of God's Spirit (Romans 12:8) needed by all Christian families and is manifested in the fellowship of believers.

The adjustment struggles of two formerly selfish singles quickly give way to the confining early years of child-rearing. Too soon elementary-schoolers become teen-agers, turning the family upside down in their quest for maturity. Then comes the silence of the empty nest as the two now middle-age parents discover what is left of their marriage.

The church provides opportunities through these changes. It preaches the Word, challenging sin and calling for a decision from every family member. It is the theater of the Spirit where the family, individually and together, encounters the living God. It is the helping hand of pastors and laypersons with counsel during crisis and confusion. It is the voice of intercessory prayer when only a miracle will meet the need. Here the scourge of divorce may be turned back and marital unity preserved.

Marriage, as God intended, is mission possible with rewards for two dedicated Christians willing to pursue it on God's terms.

Edgar Lee, S.T.D., is academic dean at Assemblies of God Theological Seminary in Springfield, Missouri.

2
IMPROVING YOUR MARRIAGE

By Glen Ryswyk

My wife, Diane, and I, along with our oldest son, heard the doctor say, "Your son has diabetes." Along with the crushing pain, agony and grief for our son, I thought: *This is the kind of stress that breaks up relationships. This is one of life's storms that rips and tears at the fabric of even stable, well-anchored relationships.*

Diane and I searched for spiritual resources to sustain us. Out of our struggle came these confirmations of biblical principles often used in counseling to improve marriages.

1. *Become more gracious to yourself.* If you are not loving and gracious toward yourself, you likely will not be loving and gracious toward your spouse. Often a marriage partner will ask a spouse to do what he/she is unwilling to do—that is, "Love me, when I don't love myself."

Jesus taught us to love our neighbors as we love ourselves. (See Mark 12:33.) When we are critical of ourselves, we will also be critical of the people we are with—our spouse and children. We cannot give what we do not have; we will give what we do have.

Both partners must live and relate from a state of grace rather than a state of law. Gracious partners do more positive reflections than critical analyses. Gracious marriages rely more on internal cohesion than on external coercion.

2. *Create an atmosphere of tolerance.* We all have an image

17

of the ideal mate, but we married an imperfect person. We can choose to cherish the image and destroy the person, or cherish the person and destroy the image.

Tolerate with humor your spouse's occasional craziness, irritability, tiredness, awkwardness, error, blues and even disagreeable viewpoint. It is the better part of forgiveness. Jesus implied that forgiveness is an ongoing process. (See Matthew 18:22.)

Tolerance doesn't mean you pretend to enjoy or be pleased by less-than-acceptable behavior. It means you express displeasure gently and kindly in an appropriate time and manner. It means most of the time you concentrate on the things you like about your spouse. "Charity suffereth long, and is kind" (1 Corinthians 13:4*).

3. *Build friendship skills.* The foundation of a strong and healthy relationship is concern for the other person's well-being and the ability to demonstrate that concern.

When annoyed by a friend's tardiness, we may say, "That's all right; don't worry about it." When nerves are worn thin by the hectic pace, a phone call from a friend elicits a warm and enthusiastic, "How are you?" Under the same conditions a spouse might get a stoic, cold and distant grunt.

People like to be around people who make them feel good. Building friendship skills means building respect for each other's differences, dreams, dignity and vulnerability. It means taking pleasure in just hanging out together. Friendship defines love into valued relationship. We are to love not only in word, but in deed and in truth. (See 1 John 3:18.)

4. *Verbalize love, acceptance and commitment.* Deep and lasting love is characterized by verbalized loyalty, acceptance, trust, caring and intimacy. Jesus, the Son of God, needed to hear His Father verbalize His love: "This is my beloved Son, in whom I am well pleased" (Matthew 3:17). We too need to hear our spouses speak love and commitment.

Security in a relationship is solidified through spoken words—"I love you," and "I will always love only you." Say

---

*All Scripture references in this chapter are from the King James Version.

wonderful things about your spouse eye-to-eye, face-to-face and heart-to-heart.

Praise your partner's character. Even out-of-balance traits have redeeming qualities. Couples who have weathered the worst storms verbalize and demonstrate their high level of commitment. Committed couples talk about marriage being worth the time, energy and effort to make it work.

5. *Grow together in communication.* Don't expect your spouse to read your mind. Be in constant contact and discussion, confiding and debating everything from work to the wash, from diapers to daily devotions. Listening to your spouse through small talk leads to understanding the thoughts of the heart. Repeat to your spouse what you have heard communicated so he/she will know feelings are important.

Feelings are often the most important concept in communication. You can know in your head you are loved; but, if you can't feel it in your heart, it doesn't mean much. Your spouse may have heard your words; but, if he or she didn't capture the feelings, the words ring hollow. He is like the man who "answereth a matter before he heareth it, it is folly and shame unto him" (Proverbs 18:13).

6. *Foster fun and laughter.* Marriages don't collapse overnight. They become bankrupt gradually because of a lack of daily deposits of fun, laughter and enjoyable experiences. "A merry heart doeth good like a medicine" (Proverbs 17:22).

Seriousness, crises and the daily grind take the place of spontaneity and romance. A night out with your partner makes the daily grind tolerable. Fun, laughter and pleasurable experiences are twice as much fun when enjoyed with the one you love.

7. *Practice fighting fair. Great marriages are not built on avoiding conflict but rather creatively handling conflict.* Follow these healthy rules: Think before you speak. Focus on one issue. Deal only with the current problem. Don't intimidate by name calling or belittling verbal jabs. Practice honesty but not brutality. Defuse explosive negative feelings before they get out of control. Attempt to describe irritating

behavior or actions, not character or personhood. Discuss to clear the air, not to win. Be willing to accept at least 50 percent of the responsibility in the misunderstanding. Focus on what you can do to make things better, rather than on what your spouse should do differently. Practice compromise and celebrate peaceful settlements.

And always remember "a soft answer turneth away wrath: but grievous words stir up anger" (Proverbs 15:1).

8. *Balance individuation and mutuality.* Individuation means finding and developing who you are, separate from your parents, spouse or children. Jesus taught that a man is to leave his father and mother before cleaving to his wife. (See Matthew 19:5.) Emotionally leave your childhood family, as well as develop a life of your own before entering the marriage or parental roles.

Find time for at least one hobby. Some independence will give you something to bring back to the relationship. Marriage will not make you happy or unhappy—it will only make you more of what you already are.

But autonomy has to be balanced with mutuality. The ability of mature couples to share the pleasant as well as the unpleasant is a mark of a healthy relationship. Share chores, ideas, concerns and goals. Share nonsexual touches—hold hands, hug, place an arm around the shoulder—that simply mean "I love you."

9. *Rehearse your memories.* Memory is a powerful tool to energize and revitalize a sagging emotional state. Remember those earlier romantic days of falling in love. Rehearse special moments of affection, times of fun and laughter. Recall the faithfulness of God. Verbally reflect on the ways your spouse has blessed you. Recount the times your spouse bailed you out of predicaments you got yourself into. Verbalize how much less you might have been if your spouse had not loved and cared for you.

10. *Share spiritual experiences.* Pray together at your church altar, in your devotions, at your bedside or in times of crisis. Share paragraphs or even entire books together. Talk about what you desire from God. Take on a project

together—care for a needy family, teach a class or do a block party to meet your neighbors.

The energy invested in improving your marriage relationship may well be your best spent energy. Long after kids are grown, careers are over and accomplishments have tarnished, you will still have a need to love and be loved. Make deposits in your spouse's love bank today.

Glen Ryswyk, M.Div., is an Assemblies of God chaplain/clinical director of Christian Family Counseling Center in Lawton, Oklahoma.

3
HAPPILY
EVER AFTER

By G. Raymond Carlson

I s the family disappearing along with yesterday's outmod-
ed styles and mores? In past generations, shelter, food,
clothing, health, birth and death were family concerns.
Now we are rapidly becoming a land of homeless, rootless,
lonely people.

Father lives and moves in his own world. Mother too has
her own agenda. Teen-agers spend most of their time with
their peers. Youngsters are in nursery school or glued to the
TV. Home becomes little more than a motel, a cafeteria and
a Laundromat.

Add to these the mobility which separates family members
from relatives, our hectic lifestyles and the hazy meaning of
parenthood, and you can see that the family is in trouble.

A Christian home should be a precursor to heaven, where
parents submit "one to another in the fear of God"
(Ephesians 5:21*). There they raise their children in the nurture and admonition of the Lord. In such a home children
obey their parents, God's Word has an honored place, prayer
time is meaningful, the Lord's Day is special and the church
is vital.

The Bible speaks clearly on the sanctity and permanence
of marriage. Christian marriage is the union of one Christian
woman to one Christian man. God's creation of the man was

*All Scripture references in this chapter are from the King James Version.

not complete until He had created a mate for him. God's Word states: "Therefore shall a man leave his father and his mother, and shall cleave unto his wife: and they shall be one flesh" (Genesis 2:24). God clearly intended permanence in marriage: "What therefore God hath joined together, let not man put asunder" (Matthew 19:6).

Family and home are related to God in inception, conception, origin and perpetuation. The home is a sort of trustee of the faith, a clearinghouse for truth. The greatest force in the life of the child is his/her home. While the family is the building block of society, the Christian family is the building block of the new society, the Church.

Marriage Strengths

A marriage must find a *mental* relationship. Open lines of communication and sharing ideas are needed.

A marriage must find a *physical* relationship. "And God said unto them, Be fruitful, and multiply, and replenish the earth" (Genesis 1:28). Life is not created in the home; it is transmitted. God created man and woman as sexual beings not only with the capacity to reproduce, but also with the capacity and desire to enjoy each other sexually, a quality distinctive to mankind. As with all gifts from God, our sexuality is not to be abused. The Bible clearly indicates that each is to limit his/her sexual relations to a spouse.

A marriage must find a *spiritual* relationship. Praying together, reading and studying God's Word together, and worshiping together are ingredients for a happy and successful marriage.

Marriage Responsibilities

The man is the head of the home (1 Corinthians 11:3; Ephesians 5:23). As head, the husband is responsible to God for his wife and children. The father is entrusted with teaching the Scriptures by word and example, directing family prayer and worship, and leading in the ways of righteousness. The father should provide materially, according to ability.

And above all, he should provide an example of a loving

relationship. Children receive security as they see their father's love and gentleness toward their mother.

The father is the protector. He'll be a good listener, seek opportunities to give his children a sense of belonging, and commend and encourage them when they do a job well or exhibit pleasing behavior. He'll find time to laugh and play with them and to help them in their difficulties.

The mother has the primary influence with the children. She is at the center of home management, which does much to contribute to their security and confidence.

Mothers—and fathers—can give the following treasures to their children:

First, a sense of law and order. Through order and discipline children learn the rights of others and how to get along. Discipline is to a young life what guardrails are to a bridge. In Jesus' home in Nazareth He learned family relationships. He had four brothers and several sisters, so there was room for misunderstanding. His brothers didn't always understand Him, and His mother didn't always comprehend Him. Understanding and adjustments were learned in their home.

Second, reverence for life. Children need to practice the Golden Rule. Respect for the body, the temple of the Holy Spirit, should be taught.

Third, appreciation for values. Appreciation for spiritual values and the family unit is vital. Children should be taught to honor their father and mother according to Exodus 20:12 and Ephesians 6:1.

Fourth, character. Goodness is not put on and taken off at a moment's notice; it is ingrained by daily living.

Fifth, the knowledge of God. The Old Testament patriarchs pitched their tents and built altars; too often today parents build their tents and pitch the altars.

Basic Principles

Here are some basic principles for building a stronger marriage and healthier home:

Play together. Did your parents have time for recreation and play with their children? If so, you count those times as treasured memories. Families who have fun together knit themselves into units that last and give opportunities to teach fairness, honesty, self-control and sportsmanship. Vacations should be planned with family members in mind.

Set tradition. The traditions in your home do not have to be something big. In fact, seemingly minor customs are often the ones that bear fruit in later years. The Bible advocates traditions: "That this may be a sign among you, that when your children ask their fathers in time to come, saying, What mean ye by these stones?" (Joshua 4:6). "And it shall come to pass, when your children shall say unto you, What mean ye by this service?" (Exodus 12:26).

Let love reign. Love has the capacity to adjust itself to the changing relationships of a home. Where love reigns and endures, there is unbeatable optimism. Love is the foundation of a happy home; good manners are the walls; diplomacy is the roof. Fill your home with good music and literature. Develop your children's appetites for the good things of life.

Worship together. Teach your children to talk to the Lord about things which are important to them. Prayer times can be at mealtimes, bedtimes, crisis times such as sickness, and at times when guests are in the home. Read Bible storybooks to small children. Develop participation at the family altar—a song, a testimony, a prayer, a question to be answered. Provide an opportunity for members to share their concerns and needs. Shun formality. Avoid monotony. Let your family altar be a simple, sincere time of fellowship with God and each other.

Someone once stated that six things are required to create a happy home: "*Integrity* must be the architect and *tidiness* the upholsterer. It must be warmed by *affection*, lighted up with *cheerfulness. Industry* must be the ventilator, renewing the atmosphere and bringing in fresh salubrity day by day; while over all, as a protecting canopy and glory, nothing will suffice except the *blessing of God.*"

G. Raymond Carlson (1918-99) served as general superintendent of the Assemblies of God from 1986 to 1993. Other offices he held included superintendent of the Minnesota District and assistant general superintendent of the Assemblies of God.

FAMILY LIFE

"But as for me and my house,
we will serve the Lord."

— Joshua 24:15 (NIV)

4
THE FAMILY ALTAR

By Juleen Turnage

Our efforts to find a regular time for family altar with our three sons often ended in frustration and failure. Getting five schedules to cooperate, especially during those teen years, was nearly impossible. And just as difficult was focusing Bible study in areas that spoke equally to all ages and interests. Yet we knew as parents this was to be a priority.

One day I read again Deuteronomy 6. The Holy Spirit spoke to my heart, "This is the key to family altar." The passage reads, "These commandments that I give you today are to be upon your hearts. Impress them on your children. Talk about them when you sit at home and when you walk along the road, when you lie down and when you get up. Tie them as symbols on your hands and bind them on your foreheads. Write them on the doorframes of your houses and on your gates" (Deuteronomy 6:6-9*).

This passage, central to Jewish faith, is known as the Shema. Jewish homes post this passage on their doorposts on a mezuzah which reminds them of their obligation to love God supremely and teach their children to love and obey Him.

*All Scripture references in this chapter are from the New International Version, except where noted.

Judaism sees God as integrated into every aspect of life. Unfortunately, we Americans have compartmentalized our lives too often into sacred and secular. But for the Christian there is no sacred and secular—every moment is lived in the presence of God. So whether I'm in the grocery store, behind the wheel of my car or in church, I'm to live in obedience to God and His Word—and teach my children to do the same.

This concept revolutionized our family altar times. If we take literally that we are to "impress them [God's command-ments] upon our children" when we sit, when we walk, when we lie down and when we get up, then we realize the family altar is not one time or place—it is a lifestyle.

Anytime, Anyplace

Now our family altar occurs throughout the day. At meal-times, we discuss the day's events, particularly those people God has brought across our paths. We focus on the Bible and principles it outlines for our response or behavior in that day's situations. These discussions, since they deal with situations we've dealt with that day, often become lengthy and take us to many different Scriptures. Our prayer times take on a new dimension as we commit ourselves to walking in obedience to the Word as we go about our daily activities.

"When you walk along the way" often is translated "as you drive in your car." We listen to Christian music or taped ser-mons. We sing along in worship and discuss what God is doing in our lives and the world. We even have times of prayer (with the driver watching and praying), and some of our most memorable family altars have been "along the way."

As I look over years of practicing a lifestyle of family altar, we have learned the following:

1. *God wants to be involved in every part of our lives.* No matter where we go, we can never flee from God's presence. (See Psalm 139.) Even in times when we don't feel His pres-ence, He's there. But this is also a sober warning that, because He is always there, we must live in ways that are

pleasing and acceptable to Him—at home, in the market-place, on the job.

2. *We must capture every moment to teach our sons and daughters the precepts of Scripture.* The Bible is our all-sufficient rule for faith and conduct, yet too often we are ignorant of its teachings. By using every opportunity that comes along to go to Scripture and see what it tells us to do, we learn line upon line and precept upon precept.

3. *We no longer struggle to find a relevant topic to capture the family's attention.* Our day's experiences provide a forum through which we seek God and His guidance. For example, when we lost a dear friend, we turned to Scripture to recall what it said about the death of believers. It reminded us that death doesn't have the final word but is the entrance into the very presence of the Lord. As we sang together songs like "He Lives" and "Because He Lives," we knew once more that Jesus has conquered death.

Another time, we discussed the Great Commandment also contained in the Deuteronomy 6 passage: "Love the Lord your God with all your heart and with all your soul and with all your strength" (v.5). Jesus quotes this passage in Matthew and expands it to "love your neighbor as yourself." Our family altar time extended for an entire evening as we discussed why the Great Commandment comes before the Great Commission and what loving God with all of our heart, soul and strength would really involve for our family.

As we gained a new perspective on practicing God's presence in our lives, Paul's admonition to the Corinthians has become our prayer: "Whether therefore ye eat, or drink, or whatsoever ye do, do all to the glory of God" (1 Corinthians 10:31, KJV).

Juleen Turnage is director of Public Relations at the Assemblies of God Headquarters.

5
MAKING CHURCH
A PRIORITY

By LeRoy Bartel

How can we keep our families involved in church? Parents frequently tell me, "Our kids want to be involved in sports, cheerleading, band or choir. How can we deal with competing work schedules? Sometimes it seems like there isn't a moment free anymore. We barely find time to eat a meal together. Sometimes our kids resent our involvement in church."

Comments like these reveal the challenges Christian families wrestle with in today's world. It's easy for young people to lose interest, become resentful and drop out of church. Families can allow the busy pace of life to force their involvement in church into the background.

But it is possible to keep the family involved in the church —joyously involved. One of the most remarkable families I know found a way. The parents were home missionaries with demanding schedules. The obligations facing the children were great. They were involved in the activities and ministries of the church—teaching Sunday school, helping with the boys and girls programs, cleaning the church and much more. The children attended public school and were involved in its activities as well. Remarkably, I never observed any resentment of their parents' ministry or the church in their lives. Instead, each of the four children exhibited a passion to discover the will of God and a desire to live it out in Christian service.

How is this possible? The answer is found in three commitments that complement and reinforce each other.

Commitment of Parents

The quality of the parents' commitment to Christ, their children and the local church is a critical issue. If the family is to be involved in ministry in the local church, the parents must lead the way with dedication and service. Their involvement in the life and ministry of the local church must be more than simply the fulfillment of a religious obligation. It must flow out of deep devotion to Christ, a love for the church and a delight in helping it fulfill its mission. Mere duty will not do—delight is the key. Complaining, criticism and cynicism poison the outlook of children. The attitude of Mom and Dad in their service for Jesus is contagious.

Parents must possess a deep conviction that God has a design and purpose for each of their children. They should consider it their God-given mission to assist their children in discovering it. Interests, abilities, passions, personality and preferences should all be considered. Encourage your children to find something they can do for the Lord that interests them and fits their makeup. Praise and affirm their endeavors more than polished performance. At the same time urge them "to do all to the glory of God" (1 Corinthians 10:31*).

Finding a ministry that your family can share together is especially gratifying. It may be cleaning the church, visiting a shut-in, hosting a backyard Bible club, distributing food to the needy or any other creative possibility. Do it with joy. "Serve the Lord with gladness" (Psalm 100:2). Plan together. Prepare together. Pray together.

Commitment of the Church

Parents need the help of the local church in raising their families. It takes a congregation to keep a family involved in church. The church is a family—a family in which God is

*All Scripture references in this chapter are from the King James Version, except where noted.

Father, Jesus is elder brother and we share care and concern for one another. The local church provides a Holy Spirit-charged context of redemptive love in which each member of the family can grow and develop in Christ. The family atmosphere of the local congregation needs to express itself in a mutual concern that does not allow anyone to become discouraged and disillusioned.

A core value that every church needs to embrace is that every believer has unique gifts to be discovered, developed and used to strengthen the church. It must take seriously its responsibility to assist people of every age in gift identification and development. It then has an obligation to help position and involve these individuals in ministries that fit them. The congregation that commits itself to this task performs a very important service for those who desire to keep their family involved in the church.

The entire congregation must recognize that it has an opportunity to foster an encouraging, affirming climate for individuals of all ages. Those involved in ministries with children and youth should look for ways to involve them. Times of consecration when gifts and abilities are dedicated to God must be valued. The church's altar should be a place where individuals of all ages can hear God's call to Christian service. The local church ought to be family-friendly in its commitment to provide transgenerational opportunities for fellowship, learning and ministry—opportunities in which the whole family can grow and serve together.

Commitment of Family Members

A commitment from parents and the church is not enough, however. Each family member needs to make his/her own commitment to Christ and His body. Additionally, family members should accept responsibility to keep each other accountable and involved.

Opportunities for commitment ought to abound in a church. Commitment is integral to Christianity. A congregational culture should be fostered that celebrates commitment and honors faithfulness in service.

Parents have an obligation to help children and youth learn stewardship of their time and talents. They should be taught to include God in their schedule and limit extracurricular involvement to make this possible. This is a core Christian discipline.

On the other hand, the commitments we expect of children and youth should be realistic. Children and youth must never be coerced or manipulated to make or live out commitments beyond normal developmental expectations. They cannot be expected to carry out responsibilities beyond their mental or emotional maturity. Nevertheless, the idealism and enthusiasm of youth in serving Jesus often surprises adults, positively influences an entire congregation and fosters revival.

How gratifying and exciting to see an entire family involved in the church—each member serving the Lord in keeping with his/her abilities. May we work together to see more families "devoted to one another, honoring one another, never lacking in zeal, keeping their spiritual fervor and serving the Lord" (adapted from Romans 12:10,11, NIV).

LeRoy Bartel is national director of the Division of Christian Education at the Assemblies of God Headquarters.

6
CONNECTING

By Bill Carmichael

A survey asked 1,500 children, "What do you think makes for a happy family?" They did not list fancy houses, more money, new cars or other status symbols.

"Doing things together" was their response. What families do is not nearly as important as the fact that they do it together.[1]

And it isn't just the fun stuff. Doing daily chores like housecleaning and yard work should be a big part of togetherness.

Today we struggle with the togetherness issue because so many voices scream for our time and attention. Family time competes with so many other things that demand attention. In this time pressure cooker, many parents end up missing out on their children's childhoods.

Raising our children is a special calling. There may only be one window of opportunity when a child will ask a certain question or one time when a teen-ager will be open to your input. If you miss that moment, it may be gone forever. Time is a nonrenewable resource; when it's gone, it's gone forever.

Your children need to feel they have you completely and exclusively once in a while. They need to sense by your actions that they are the most important person in the world to you. This is not something you give your children as an option. It is vital to their healthy development and their sense of self-worth.[2] We must connect with them in three areas:

1. _Connecting through touch._ Appropriate touch is an important way of connecting. Several studies show that infants who are touched, cuddled and held, sleep better, gain necessary weight better and are healthier than babies who are not touched by a loving caregiver. Loving touch communicates security and builds children's self-esteem.

Hugging is like a miracle drug. It reduces stress, assists the body's immune system and induces sleep. It makes us feel loved and cared for. Hugging melts hostilities and fosters closeness. It is a vital part of connection and togetherness.

2. _Connecting through commitment._ To ensure our children's sense of connection and belonging, we must remember that the stability of our marriage relationship affects our children for their entire lives. Good marriages take hard work. Good marriages are something we do. It is a matter of the heart. It is understanding the meaning of commitment. Working hard to create love and harmony is a choice we must make every day if we want our children to have a sense of connection and wholeness.

3. _Connecting through grace._ Sometimes a little grace at the right time will not only strengthen the connection between you and your child, but also point his/her life in the right direction forever. It is better to bind your children to you through acts of mercy and grace than it is through acts of fear and punishment.

Don't be afraid to ask for grace. When you make a mistake, ask your family for some grace. Some parents feel it is a sign of weakness to repent and ask for forgiveness, when in reality it is a sign of strength. How else can your children learn about grace and repentance if they don't see you dip into its solace once in a while? Your acts of repentance will bond and connect your children to you in a powerful way and put a needed nutrient into the good ground of your home.

The most conspicuous threat to family togetherness is found in nearly every family room: the television. In some homes, it has turned the family from a close-knit unit into a disjointed collection of individuals. It is important for parents to remember that television has a tendency to destroy a family's interaction with each other.

We teach our children what is valuable by the way we spend our time. Television is addictive. It can steal our time.

Showing Compassion

One of the most wonderful ways to connect with your children is by doing things together for others, expecting nothing in return. Something wonderful happens when you reach out to help others, to see the needs of others as more important than your own.

Our children need to know how to give to others; how to be compassionate; how to identify with the poor, the elderly and the disadvantaged. They need to appreciate what struggles others may have to endure just to survive. Home is where we can learn the concept of compassion and charity.

Charlotte Lunsford, national chairperson of volunteers for the Red Cross, says, "When people begin volunteering [for service] at a young age, normally they volunteer throughout their lives." Parents can cultivate the good ground of their homes by making them places that demonstrate Christ's compassion.

Home is the school for building relationships. Home teaches us how to get along and how to connect with others.

[1]Nick Stinnett and John DeFrain, "Six Secrets of Strong Families," *Reader's Digest* (November 1994): 132-135.

[2]Ross Campbell, *How To Really Love Your Child* (Wheaton, Ill.: Victor Books, 1982), 60-61.

Bill Carmichael and his wife, Nancie, are founding publishers of *Christian Parenting Today* magazine.

7
FAMILY NIGHT

By Dean Merrill

During the late 20th century there lived a sincere Christian couple with 2.4 children. The husband and wife enjoyed the usual amenities of modern living; but, unlike some of their neighbors, they were loyal adherents of a faith called Christianity.

"We want our kids to grow up to love God," they said. Toward that end, they made sure the household was up early on Sunday (the appointed day of worship) and that the children arrived at church in time for classes. They gave their money to support the church; and when the wife brought home the children's books and recordings from the Christian bookstore, the husband complained not at all about the cost.

The years went by, and in time the children fulfilled their parents' wishes, one even becoming a minister.

By now you have figured out the above story is a fable. Raising a new generation of Christians is a complicated enterprise—more complicated than any of us dreamed back at the start of the first pregnancy—and there are few guarantees.

My wife, Grace, and I certainly had few strategies in place when our firstborn arrived. His twin sisters came (with only 10 days' notice there would be two) a couple of years later. In those early days we were both so busy changing diapers and tugging with snowsuits that we thought only fleetingly about spiritual development. We read them bedtime books about Jesus, of course, and sprinkled the days with Christian music. But we hardly had the energy to consider an overall plan. There would be plenty of time later.

We were bumped off dead center when Nathan trotted off to kindergarten one fall and struck up a friendship with Derek, who lived on the other side of our block. Derek's family was Mormon. We found that out the day Grace called Mrs. Van Orden and invited Derek over to play the following Monday afternoon.

"No, Derek isn't free after school on Mondays," she kindly replied. "That's our Family Home Evening. All the children go to the ward meetinghouse for clubs in the late afternoon, and then we spend the evening together as a family."

That did it. It was time for us to put our actions where our convictions were.

We invited the Van Ordens over for dessert one night, mainly to quiz them about what they did on Mondays. Here were modern, suburban parents (he was a successful display designer in downtown Chicago) who talked excitedly about the games, food, projects and teaching they enjoyed with their children every seven days.

After they left, we began to lay our own plans.

Advent was coming, and it gave us the launch we needed. Each week we gathered around the wreath, lit the candles, and talked and sang about Jesus' coming to earth. Nathan was 5; Rhonda and Tricia were 2½, and mesmerized by the flickering light. We mixed in some other activities and gave it a name: Home Together Night. When January came, we continued.

And for the next 14 years, Home Together Night was a regular part of our children's lives because we believe:

- That modern families are split up most of the week, each person going his or her separate way, and that families need to be together at least a few quality hours each week to preserve unity.

- That a child's spiritual input ought not to come entirely from outsiders. Thank God for pastors, Sunday school teachers, club leaders and all the rest—but their efforts are not enough. No matter how much they talk, the child still questions: *I wonder what my folks think about all this? Preachers and teachers are supposed to spout all this God stuff—that's their job. But does my dad buy this? My mom?* Parental silence may mean consent, but consent is not enough to make a difference in a kid's value system. We have to say some things.
- That kids are worth a block of uninterrupted, quality time each week.
- That Christian truth can be alive and effective and can blend with other forms of family sharing. It doesn't have to be closeted off in a holy zone of formality.
- That the family is the perfect size for effective teaching. The adult-child ratio is enough to make an educator drool. What Sunday school teacher wouldn't love this setting compared to 20 moving targets?
- That the generation gap can be bridged if we really care and are willing to reach out. The words of Derek's father kept echoing in our minds: "The prophets of our church have promised us that if we give our children this time each week as they're growing up, we won't lose them when they're teen-agers. We will have built up a bank of trust to carry us through the later years."

In our house we dedicated Tuesdays as our special evening, from the time Dad arrived home from work until the kids went to bed. It meant adjusting our adult patterns, but could we honestly stand before God someday and claim we couldn't carve two or three hours out of 168 per week for concentrated parenting?

The options from which we built each Home Together Night varied. The only constants were the meal and the spiritual sharing/teaching; the others came and went. Here are some possible ingredients:

Food. The evening began with a good meal—good by a

kid's definition. Hamburgers instead of liver. Pizza instead of casserole.

The location of the meal varied, from outdoor picnics to the pingpong table to the dining room for china and candlelight. One night we carted the food to somebody's bedroom. A blanket in the front of the fireplace served the same purpose. One night Grace stunned us all by withholding silverware; it was fingers or nothing. Fortunately the menu was fried chicken, french fries, finger Jell-O, relishes and cupcakes.

The best meal, however, frustrates a child if the conversation swirls over his/her head. Therefore, we decided that table talk would be exclusively kid talk on Tuesday evening. No office politics. No heavy financial discussion. Instead, school talk, baseball talk, jokes, riddles, news about friends and bikes and dogs and dolls.

At one point Grace filled a green Tupperware container with a hundred or more questions written on the backs of my outdated business cards: "The funniest person I ever met was . . . ." "What's your favorite place on earth?" "Name something you especially enjoy at church." "What do you think parents should not do?" Virtually every week the green jar went around the table along with the Jell-O and carrot sticks. Each person took a card and started a new round of answers (five rounds in all at our house—one for each family member).

Games. Games are parables of life. They teach us in visible ways about competing, concentrating, bearing down, not giving up, winning, losing—all vital lessons for the real world. Therefore, family members playing games together enjoy one another and learn how to respond to life's realities.

The choice of games varied from Go Fish to Bible Challenge to Monopoly to soccer to catch to Frisbee, depending on the weather and the kids' preferences.

Excursions. Too many families think only of $150 extravaganzas to an amusement park, which few can afford more than once a year. Meanwhile, they miss the fun of a trip to an ice-cream shop, a band concert in the park, a toboggan slide, the public library, a hike around a lake. Nearly every area has places the average family hasn't gotten around to seeing yet, and most of them are free.

Spiritual sharing and teaching. Sometimes during the course of the evening we would take 10 minutes—often in a circle on the floor and therefore called Circle Time—for Christian input. Again the possibilities are endless, from stories, skits and pantomimes to serious Bible study with older children.

It's important that these minutes not be led exclusively by one parent or the other. Kids need to see that faith is real to both Dad and Mom.

The best times have been when we've capitalized on something happening in our children's lives. One night when the news was filled with a madman on the loose tampering with over-the-counter medicine packages, we talked about why our world has killers in it, and why others were trying to mimic the treachery. Aren't people trustworthy? We read Psalm 14, which explains how our world has been basically ruined. Then we read Psalm 15 and reviewed the way God wants us to live, even in a twisted society. Finally came the hard question: Could we pray for the killer? We didn't feel like it emotionally, but after a pause we bowed our heads together.

Outreach. You can make cookies and take them to a neighbor who is ill. You can ask to sing in nursing homes. You can make homemade cards for those in hospitals.

Praying. Keep prayer natural, conversational and tailored to the length children will appreciate rather than dread. At times, a prayer log kept us organized, helping us list our requests and rejoice when we checked them off.

Music. Every member's instrumental ability can be put to use without embarrassment. Singing fits well not only at home but also in the car.

Snacks. Popcorn or homemade ice cream can finish the evening. (For laughs, leave the lid off the popcorn popper and let the kernels fly all over a sheet on the floor.)

As you can see, we mixed the secular with the sacred, the fun with the religious. That was intentional. We didn't want our kids putting God in a Sunday/church box. We wanted them bumping into Him every time they turned around, in the midst of ordinary living.

Two rules served us well:

1. Whatever we did, we did together—the five of us. We would do only those things that all family members considered enjoyable.

For instance, Dean and Grace might like to stroll through a shopping mall looking for furniture. At one point Nathan's favorite game was Monopoly, but it was complicated for the twins. Hence, both of these activities were out of bounds on Home Together Night.

2. We would not tolerate distractions. Hence, the TV was off (unless there was a program all of us would enjoy), and the phone went unanswered. Even kitchen cleanup waited.

At times weather messed us up, forcing us to Plan B. Most often when Home Together Night faltered, however, it was because the two adults failed to think things through in advance, and chaos moved into the vacuum.

Parents must believe in Home Together Night strongly enough to sit down together 24 hours in advance and say, "What should we do this week? What does the Lord want us to emphasize?" The couple can keep a collection of resources —books, clippings—to spark their planning.

A United States senator, in the midst of debate over school prayer legislation, was speaking at a church men's breakfast. He told his audience about what was happening on the Senate floor and then asked how many were in favor of classroom prayer. Most hands went up.

"Let me ask one more question," he said. "How many of you here have prayed aloud with your children at home in the last week?" The response could be tallied on two hands. We have no right to ask public school teachers—or private ones, for that matter, or clergy, or anyone else—to do what we ourselves neglect.

Dean Merrill has written numerous books and articles. He lives in Colorado Springs, Colorado.

8

MAKING THE MOST OF LEISURE TIME

By David B. Crabtree

There is no more destructive influence on physical and mental health than the isolation of you from me and us from them."

So said psychiatrist Philip Zimbardo.

Nowhere is his assessment more obvious and ominous than in the American family. With all of our technology and discovery we've lost true fellowship. When I was a kid, we would all sing, laugh, talk and squabble as we motored down the highway to some vacation destination. Now everybody has his or her own personal listening device or escape route. Dad is on the cell phone. Mom is into her book. Johnny is zoned out with Nintendo. And Suzie is captive to her Walkman.

Tube Time

When a person is given a day to fill at home, the television or computer plays a prominent role. It's company while getting dressed in the morning; a constant voice in an empty home; a cheap baby-sitter for all age groups; a grand entertainer; a tranquilizer; a sleeping pill; a late-night companion; a window on the world; a time filler.

In most homes we have two. We only adopted this family

47

member in 1946; but in a generation it moved from the family room to the bedroom, and then invited twins to move into our living rooms and kitchens. We used to have to communicate . . . to interact . . . to entertain one another. Now we have television. It comes as standard equipment on the new model of the American family. We might not have a couple extra hours for the kids, an afternoon to volunteer at the church or even a few minutes for the spouse, but we have lots of time for television.

The tube burns 55 hours per week in the average American household equipped with cable. Where cable is not available, television is cut to 47 hours. Add to that all the time we spend interacting with a computer or game screen, and we are dealing with a medium that eats up to three days out of every seven. Technocrats are telling us that the future is online.

There's not that much time left to hijack.

We have witnessed an explosion in entertainment options, yet we are not entertained. Most channel surfers can take a complete tour of 50-plus channels during a two-minute commercial break. Some people watch two shows at once by flipping back and forth with every commercial. Some buy sets with "picture in picture" technology so that they can watch two things at once. The newspaper delivers a fat section of television news and programming each Sunday. Many of us scan the list and lament, "There's nothing on TV tonight."

Noise-Filled Hours

We fill every moment with some kind of noise. The sweet hour of prayer is filled with somebody's teaching tape. Bible reading and meditation have been cast aside for Scripture on tape during drive time. We want our religion bite-sized in a resealable package. It's no wonder that Christians complain of a lack of intimacy with God. Intimacy requires the whole heart, and our culture is geared towards multi-tasking.

What, then, shall we do? How can we preserve the family in a decaying culture? How can we pin down the online octopus? How can we learn to talk again, laugh again, play again . . . pray again?

A Simple Solution

A few weeks ago I slipped away from our campfire to walk through a Smoky Mountain campground just after sunset. I was amazed by a consistent scene: families—that's right, the whole bunch—sitting around picnic tables and campfires talking. All ages, shapes, sizes, backgrounds—laughing and talking. Then it hit me. They've unplugged it all. They simply disconnected and found what they had been missing . . . something called family.

Maybe you need to get away from it all with your family —unplug it all to reestablish vital connections. Everyone benefits from a change of scenery and airing out the mind.

The secret to a great getaway has little to do with destination, weather, luxuries or budgets. The secret lies in the packing . . . knowing what to take along and what to leave behind.

Leave behind your labors. You can't get a new grip on the thing you're unwilling to lay aside. Great ideas are born when problems are given a rest. Great works of art require downtime for the paint to dry. Great books come from partial manuscripts that were abandoned for a season. Great vision is only possible when we have distanced ourselves to see a panorama. The man or woman who thinks a few days' rest constitutes a waste of time is like the lumberjack who won't stop chopping to sharpen the axe—the harder they work, the smaller the return.

We cannot know true rest until we stop worshiping our work.

Leave behind relationships. Great friendships are strengthened by an occasional absence. See your getaway as an opportunity to open the windows and let some fresh air and fresh insight into relationships.

When we pack up all our hurts and pains and conflicts, just dragging them along, we poison the healing streams of leisure. Take a break from your bitterness, your anger and your frustrations. You may find that you don't want to pick up that nasty little trio when you get back home.

Leave behind your schedule. That tyrant has ruled you long enough. You need open-ended days that make room for the better thoughts, the better moments, the better pursuits that God has been holding for the day He can have your undivided attention. A clean slate invites all kinds of wonderful opportunities.

Once you've tossed these things aside, you need to make a short list of things to take along.

Take along your Bible. If you want to get away for a season of refreshing, you're going to need proper nourishment along the way. Don't try to survive on devotional "twinkies." You've been filling your mind with the *Journal* and the *Times*; why not fill your heart with the uplifting, life-giving, refreshing, reviving Word of God? Choose an epistle, a gospel, a theme or a character to trace throughout your journey.

Take along a spirit of adventure. Surprise your family with your availability, flexibility and adaptability. Make sure you hear somebody say, "We've never done that before," at least once along the way.

New places invite new experiences. Don't eat at the same fast-food chains or visit the same stores in carbon-copy shopping malls. You don't have to go to extremes; but whatever you do, avoid that yawning predictability that had the whole family begging for a change of venue in the first place.

Take along laughter. If you're going to have a time to remember, you had better loosen up. I once drove 200 miles with my jaws clenched over getting away later than I had planned. It is amazing the cleansing that flows from laughter . . . especially when you are laughing at yourself.

Our first priority in life should be to grow closer to God. This will require unhurried solitude. Be certain that you take time for meditation, reflection and worship. Jesus loved His disciples and He loved the seekers and He loved the little children, but He took time to get away from them to spend time with the Father. He so strongly bore the markings of those hours spent with God that the disciples asked Him to teach them to pray that they might know such peace and rest.

I'm learning to pack lighter with each getaway. It's one of the later lessons I've learned in life: the less you drag along, the less you have to carry.

David B. Crabtree is pastor of Calvary Assembly of God in Greensboro, North Carolina.

9

THE SINGLE-PARENT FAMILY

By John Kie Vining

Soon, if today's trends continue, well over one-half of all children in the United States will spend at least part of their childhood in a single-parent family. Those who will live in a blended family are likely to experience a family breakup two or three times.

Four areas of one's life can be impacted significantly by this type of loss.

First, one is affected mentally. Questioning why and placing blame cause mental pain. Attempts to figure out what happened are draining. Efforts to fix the brokenness become stressful. Often sufferers of this type of loss will complain of headaches and describe themselves as being emotionally wrung out. Loss makes thinking and feeling difficult.

Second, one's social life is affected. Relatives may not understand and be supportive. Friends may tend to stay away. Meeting new friends becomes somewhat risky because those suffering loss already feel vulnerable. Often, single-parent families have to find new housing, new schools, new jobs and sometimes new churches. Or, one simply may not feel like socializing.

Third, one's physical body suffers consequences. Appetite may diminish. Sleeping patterns may be disrupted. Energy may wane. Significant weight loss or weight gain can occur. Often there is also a lack of affectionate and meaningful touch, as the body reacts to loss.

Fourth, one's spiritual self can also be affected. A crisis of faith pushes one to doubt his/her spiritual beliefs and previous experiences. Often people ask: *What have I done to deserve this? Is God punishing me? Are my prayers being heard by God? If God is with me why doesn't He help me out of this crisis?* When a believer does not feel close to God, he/she can face a crisis of faith.

The mental, social, physical and spiritual losses lead to a sense of instability. Nothing seems sure. Both adults and children face this uncertainty. Work and school are two places where this change becomes very obvious. Sometimes this change is only in perception; other times, the change is literal.

Working Through

Grief is normal during loss; however, grief must be dealt with in order for a person to be able to get on with life. Grief work involves the following tasks that help facilitate healing:

1. *Admit that loss has occurred.* The following feelings are normal and must be expressed: guilt, remorse, apathy, anger, resentment, yearning, despair, anxiety, emptiness, depression, loneliness, panic, disorientation, loss of clear identity, physical symptoms.

2. *Accept the loss.* One must begin putting one's life back together by making decisions, discarding old ways of satisfying needs and learning new methods, and reinvesting one's energy in other relationships.

3. *Embrace your personhood in spite of loss.* The loss must be put into the wider context of faith.

4. *Seek God's direction for life after loss.* The person must begin seeking help from others who have experienced similar loss.

When people experience loss and grief, they need human compassion.

Family members in single-parent families can feel hopeless at times. The pain is unbearable. The future is bleak. But in

the sight of God and in the company of His church, there is
healing and hope for brighter days.

Hope brings comfort when one can affirm that in the view
of God and compassionate friends the following statements
are true: I am loved; I am not abandoned; I am not abnor-
mal; I am not doomed to failure; I am ultimately in God's
hands. And, remember, "He gives strength to the weary and
increases the power of the weak" (Isaiah 40:29, NIV).

Surviving Risks

As a single parent, you can survive risks by considering the
following:

1. *Accept yourself.* God made you and accepts you.

2. *Study.* Read to understand your new role as a person, as
well as a parent. Seminars, support groups and community
agencies are available. Hold yourself responsible for new
growth and direction.

3. *Monitor your physical health.* Do not neglect nutritional
needs or medical and dental checkups, but be careful not to
become overanxious about your health.

4. *Avoid excessive guilt feelings.* Vent your fears and voice
your needs to your pastor or a Christian friend. A Christian
counselor can help you work on these and other feelings.

5. *Make financial adjustments.* Mistakes in judgment may
be made if you try to adjust too quickly; on the other hand,
delays may be costly. Changing recreation habits, refraining
from eating out or selling a car or a boat may be some areas
for budget rearrangements. Job training or refresher courses
may be necessary to make the adjustment.

6. *Learn to spread out your dependencies.* For the single-
again adult, learning to diffuse dependencies can be a big
adjustment. The lawyer, counselor, minister, doctor, banker,
relatives and friends all may share in this transfer of dependencies, as the single-again person seeks to maintain his or
her identity and not lean upon others in a self-destructive
manner.

7. *Maintain wholesome relationships.* Invite people into

your home, participate in church and community life, and maintain a wholesome relationship with relatives. To cure loneliness, seek fulfilling relationships with others.

8. *Include your children in plans about the future*—residence, school, employment, income, allowances, etc. Their input creates an opportunity to express their feelings, hopes and fears. Be careful not to overburden them.

9. *Don't allow your children to feel responsible for what has happened.* In the case of divorce, avoid playing the child against the other parent. The absent parent's access to the child is important and often is a major factor in building something of value into the life of the child.

10. *Stay attuned to your child's emotional needs.* Do not smother the child with oversolicitous care. Do not make strong emotional demands to which a child is simply not mature enough to respond. Offer your companionship and love. Entertainment is no substitute for that.

11. *Maintain contact with both sets of your children's grandparents, if possible.*

12. *Enroll the children in church clubs and community youth organizations.*

13. *Make family prayer a daily experience.* Mention your children by name and share your family needs with the Lord.

14. *Delegate responsibilities around the home.* Safeguards may be needed for children who would accept too much responsibility for their level of maturity.

15. *Exercise the same discipline methods that were used in a two-parent home.* Discipline includes what is permitted as well as what is prohibited.

16. *Get help from counselors and from books and seminars.* Study child-rearing skills and personality development.

By confronting the deficits and nurturing the assets of single-parent families, children and their single parents can live happy and productive lives.

John Kie Vining, D.Min., is a licensed professional counselor.

PARENTING

"Parents . . . raise [your children] properly.
Teach them and instruct them
about the Lord."

— Ephesians 6:4 (CEV)

10
HELPING CHILDREN KNOW GOD

By Richard D. Dobbins

Your God-concept is a combination of images, feelings and thoughts that give you an understanding of God. It becomes the lens through which you see God and through which you believe God sees you.

This God-concept remains buried and distorted to some extent, regardless of how spiritually mature we may be, because it is the product of our mental limitations. Still, the nature of the God-concept acquired in childhood not only tends to attract us to God or repel us from God; that concept also affects our comfort and productivity.

Why Is the God-Concept Important?

When we contribute to a healthy God-concept in a child, we contribute to the child's lifelong productivity.

We interact with God through the concept we have of Him. No other idea exerts such a powerful influence on believers' lives as their God-concept. On the spiritual side, it is the difference between duty and discovery; between fear and love. On the physical side, it is the difference between being tense and being relaxed.

Your God-concept tends to stabilize over time and resists change. You think about God today much as you did 10 years ago. Your ideas of Him do not change automatically because you are a Christian. If you were afraid of Him when you were an unbeliever, you will probably be afraid of Him now that you are a Christian.

Many Christians cannot believe God loves them. They know what they know about themselves, and they don't love themselves. So they question how God, who knows all, could love them.

As I deal with emotionally disturbed believers, there are two main points for therapy: the self-concept and the God-concept. I work more with the God-concept, because a person cannot have a healthy view of God and sick view of self. The God-concept is more readily accessible because it is formed later in the developmental process.

Early relationships with parents influence the nature of the child's God-concept. If his earthly father is patient, loving and kind, he tends to see his Heavenly Father as patient, loving and kind. If her earthly father tells her he is pleased with her and expresses affection, she tends to believe that most of the time her Heavenly Father is pleased with her and loves her even when He is not pleased.

If an earthly father is hard to please, impatient, and angry much of the time, his children see God as hard to please, impatient and angry. The attitude of children toward their earthly father colors their view of their Heavenly Father; thus, Paul admonished earthly fathers to nurture their children. (See Ephesians 6:4.)

When Is the God-Concept Formed?

David Elkind, in a study reported in 1971, defines the period of development in which the child's God-concept comes into focus by tracing religious behavior following growth stages.

He talks about *prepersonal religious behaviors.* These are religiouslike behaviors the infant displays toward the parent that later may be transferred to the child's concept of God. Examples of prepersonal religious behaviors are love, trust, fear, comfort, joy, awe and respect. These are experiences children can know with their earthly parents before they have any idea who God is.

Then Elkind talks about *institutional religious behaviors and experiences.* These are introduced to children by the institutional church. Before they are a year old or shortly after that, children can be taught to fold their hands and bow their heads.

Third, Elkind refers to *personal religious experiences and behaviors.* These are acquired, spontaneous experiences discovered by children when they apply their institutional and prepersonal religious experiences to life situations. They often occur at boys and girls camps or youth camps. The God of Mom and Dad becomes the God of son or daughter.

Sometimes people are in late adolescence or early adulthood before they have a personal faith. But at some point, Elkind says, if they are spiritually healthy and mature, they will experience God for themselves.

How Is the God-Concept Formed?

An accumulation of ideas and feelings about God from all sources begins to coalesce and define itself in the child's understanding of who God is. This gradually comes into focus about age 5 and is well-defined by age 7.

About the time children discover that their parents don't know and can't do everything, they need to believe there is Someone who does. This is the root of the God-concept. In this crisis in early childhood, a process is working to form the God-concept in children. Expectations no longer held of parents are projected onto God.

In Matthew 18:6 Jesus warns His disciples of the serious consequences of spiritually offending children. Early impressions tend to be lasting ones. He knew that children's impressions of adults become the foundation of their God-concept. Parents who turn children off to themselves risk turning those children off to God.

The more knowledgeable we are of how the God-concept is formed and the more committed we are to building that

God-concept as healthy and strong as possible, the less likely our children will grow up to face tomorrow with twisted and distorted ideas about God.

Parents and teachers, be sure you present to children a God they can live with throughout their lives.

Richard D. Dobbins, Ph.D., an Assemblies of God minister, is founder and director of Emerge Ministries, Inc., a counseling center in Akron, Ohio.

11
INSTILLING CHRISTIAN VALUES

By Glen D. Cole

Parenting demands the best we can give. Here are eight principles for instilling values in your children that will last a lifetime:

Give your children proper parental affection. In the preverbal years, how much time do you think an average father spends with his child per day? Less than 30 seconds! Does that say that fathers don't like to get involved with diaper changing and feeding? If that continues, think of the effect it's going to have upon the child.

Fathers can make a valuable contribution in the area of affection. If they do not, how is that going to affect the children in relation to others? For example, the police, the teacher, the pastor. What will be the children's reaction to God if they don't have the affection of their earthly fathers? No closeness. No father figure that means anything. If we're going to instill in our children proper attitudes for life, it's got to start from the very beginning.

Spend time with your children. What do the majority of American families spend time doing these days? Sitting in front of the television. What's more important, quality time or quantity time?

Our busyness, our involvements take away from the quantity. But if we were to choose, we would have to choose quality. If we're going to instill values in our children, we must learn to plan together and play together and pray together.

Discipline your children. It's frightening for a youngster to discover he/she is in charge. It's like being in a car with no brakes. Where do the brakes come from? Parents. Be willing to say no as well as yes.

Parents, be willing to risk the wrath of the child at times. Look at Proverbs 22:15*: "Foolishness is bound in the heart of a child; but the rod of correction shall drive it far from him." Proverbs 13:24 says: "He who spares the rod hates his son, but he who loves him is careful to discipline him" (NIV).

Live a positive, joyful life. A counselor suggested to a mother, whose 11-year-old son was failing nearly every subject, that she listen carefully to every word she said to him for one day. When she did, she was appalled. "I had no idea I only spoke to Jimmy to admonish him or order him to do something," she said.

Dad, you've been busy all day long, and now you're going home. What should be your attitude when you walk through that door? Joyful. Who wants to have a grouch come home? Certainly not children, who are so full of life. Leave problems outside the door. Be upbeat when you walk in.

Remember, "the joy of the Lord is your strength" (Nehemiah 8:10). Make your home environment positive and happy.

Keep promises to your children. If you say, "If you do that once more, you're going to get a spanking!" and the child does it once more, keep your word.

Or, consider this: You say, "On Saturday we're going to take a picnic and go to the park." Saturday comes. What should you do? Short of a hurricane, go to the park. Children need to believe what you say.

Why do we have a generation that is somewhat rebellious toward the church? It's because rebellion is in the home. Parents say, "I'm going to do this," and they don't. They fail to build into their children respect for God, the policeman, the teacher—and themselves.

---

*All Scripture references in this chapter are from the King James Version, except where noted.

Missionary David Grant says, "We all need some 'I can hardly waits' in our calendar." We need something we're reaching for, looking forward to. Children need that, and they need you to keep your promise.

Don't speak negatively about Christian leaders. Going through negative things publicly regarding ministry affects all of us. How much more so for an impressionable little mind sitting at a table with us every day?

When parents give their children only negatives, the children too will speak negatively of God and His work. So keep it positive.

Don't make fun of your children. I've seen this happen. Self-esteem is the cornerstone for good mental health. Some parents are always putting their children down, saying, "You're bad. You're naughty"—or worse. What are you going to raise? You're going to raise exactly what you've said. So don't make fun of your children. Don't put them down. Lift them up. That's the parents' responsibility. If we're going to instill the right things in them, it's got to be on that basis. Pick out the good points.

Train your children to be courteous and friendly. If they're trained that way, they're going to influence others, and it's going to affect our society for good. Teach them to respect the opinions and rights of other people, to respect elders and teachers, pastors, and government leaders.

"Train up a child in the way he should go: and when he is old, he will not depart from it" (Proverbs 22:6). I'm glad I am bearing the fruit of that right now. You will be glad, too. Values. We need to pass them on. They will help us to bring up people who are going to touch other people for Christ. That's what it's all about.

Glen D. Cole is superintendent of the Northern California-Nevada District of the Assemblies of God.

12
TEACHING CHILDREN TO PRAY

By Marjorie Gordon

J esus, I hope You come again while I'm little, so I can play Superman all the way to heaven," prayed 4-year-old Ryan. His parents had taught him to "just talk to Jesus."

When I was growing up, my bedtime ritual included praying, "Now I lay me down to sleep; I pray the Lord my soul to keep." My table prayer was, "God is great. God is good. Let us thank Him for our food." Now I realize these were the only signs of godliness in my childhood home. They impressed on me that God was my keeper and provider, but no one taught me the possibilities of prayer.

We need to understand what prayer is so we can teach our children to pray. It is an invitation from God to talk with Him in two-way conversation. God's part may be words from the Bible or a quiet voice in our thoughts. Our part should be as varied and enjoyable as talking with a good friend who is able to help us in every situation. Prayer is the evidence of a relationship between God and His children.

Consider five factors in teaching children to pray.

1. *Introduce children personally to Jesus.* When Corrie ten Boom was 5, her mother overheard her knocking on a make-believe door. She said, "Corrie, I know Someone who is standing at your door and knocking right now. Jesus said that He is standing at the door, and if you invite Him in He will come into your heart. Would you like to invite Jesus in?"

She remembered the incident well after many years.

Her mother impressed her to pray for others by telling her she was an intercessor. She recalled walking through her neighborhood praying for neighbors. Years later, she learned of many who had come into a personal relationship with Jesus. Never discount the potential of children's prayers.

I introduced my first grandchild, Holly, to Jesus when she was 5. I explained, "Now you are an intercessor, Holly. That's someone who can pray to God for other people."

I shouldn't have been surprised when she told me she was inviting children at school to meet with her so she could pray for them. She said, "I felt like a grown-up, Grandma, when I prayed for my friend whose mama and daddy are getting a divorce."

2. *Become role models.* What we teach our children about prayer flows from our own relationship with God.

Susanna Wesley, mother of 17 children, is reported to have kept her daily prayer time by sitting in her chair with her apron thrown over her head. What a powerful message about God and prayer she gave her children. Little wonder her sons, Charles and John Wesley, became founders of the Methodist church.

Do your children hear you speaking spontaneously to God throughout the day? "Good morning, God. Thank You for a new day." "God, You sure make pretty roses." Do they hear their parents praying together? You're teaching your children about prayer without realizing it.

Start early. If you make a habit of praying over your infant at bedtime, when he or she becomes a toddler, the prayer time will include the child's participation. If it is before a meal, you might hear, "Thank You, Jesus, for milk and bananas and peanut-butter sammiches."

Holding hands around the table not only provides a sense of affection, but it keeps tiny hands out of mischief.

Encourage specific prayers. In the simplicity of children's prayers we can learn about the importance of praying specifically.

God seems to delight in answering children's prayers—

perhaps because their faith is not clouded by adult logic. Suffering in the hot car on a long trip, Grant, 3, pleaded, "Mommy, I need wain."

She flippantly said, "Ask Jesus."

Grant pointed all around and said, "Jesus, please give me some wain." Five minutes later huge raindrops pelted the car.

3. *Encourage conversational prayer.* Children often direct their prayers to Jesus. Allow them to continue the relationship which begins when they invite Him to come into their hearts. If they hear us talking to our Heavenly Father or to the Holy Spirit in addition to Jesus, they have little trouble relating to the Trinity. My second grader revealed this when he wrote in a school paper, "Christmas is God's birthday. If you don't think this is so, just ask my mother."

A mother overheard this conversation from her child who had slammed her finger in the door: "Jesus, please heal my finger, but wait until my daddy comes home and sees it."

4. *Include Scripture promises.* Jeremiah 1:12 tells us God watches over His Word to see that it is fulfilled. When we include His Word in our prayers, we are praying in His will. "Thank You, Heavenly Father, that You give Your angels charge of Larry to guard him in all his ways." "Thank You, God, that You never slumber or sleep. That means You'll be awake to take care of Michelle while she sleeps." Prayers like these help children become better acquainted with God and increase their confidence in Him.

5. *Add variety.* A prayer can be a song or a Scripture reading. Families can use prayer times to learn the Lord's Prayer. Avoid using the same words and expressions repeatedly. Pray in words children understand. If your prayers change in style often, so will your children's.

Jan realized the effectiveness of teaching her children to pray when Breanna placed her hands squarely on her hips and demanded, "Where is Jesus?" Jan explained He was in heaven, but He was also in her heart. Breanna continued, "Well, I want to talk to Him now. I want to ask Him why I have to obey."

I wish someone had taught me I could just talk to God. I

wouldn't have spent so many years praying, "Now I lay me down to sleep."

Marjorie Gordon, a nurse, lives in Auburn, Washington.

13
TEACHING CHILDREN TO GIVE

By Billie Davis

I was good," Ken announced to his mother's friends who were riding home from church with his family. "I gave part of my birthday money in the missionary offering."

"Now don't go bragging," scolded his mother. "It's not nice to brag about yourself like that."

Ken's mother made a common error. She thought in adult terms about the actions of a child. Ken was not bragging. Of course neither he nor his mother knew it, but he was expressing what some psychologists say is the purest pleasure humans can feel. He was living up to his values. He had been taught to give, and now giving was a pleasure.

No biblical principle is more clearly stated than the importance of giving—from giving bread to the poor to giving one's life for the Lord. "It is more blessed to give than to receive" (Acts 20:35*) is a kind of moral statement, but also it says something about human nature.

Sometimes adults who teach the Bible passage do not fully understand it. They seem to present the act of giving as a duty, a sacrifice, rather than as the joy indicated by Scripture. Another word for blessed is happy. The Good News Bible puts it like this: "There is more happiness in giving than in receiving."

*All Scripture references in this chapter are from the King James Version, except where noted.

People experience happiness—pleasure, contentment, gladness, joy—when their greatest needs are fulfilled. Among the universal human traits is a need to feel good about one's own actions. What the psychologists say is simply a secular statement of biblical truth. To allow humans the possibility of salvation, God endowed them with a sense of right and wrong. Giving brings happiness because it reflects the joy of pleasing God.

Giving is a shared pleasure. Giver and receiver both feel the blessing, and sharing experiences are uplifting to them both. Giving helps us think of others. It helps us make friends. It helps us do things together, like building churches.

The Bible teaches two specific kinds of giving that bring joy and satisfaction to Christians. One is giving that sustains the church. God made the plan called tithing as a way of caring for those who did His special service. This is explained in the laws of Moses (Leviticus 27:30,34; Numbers 18:21; Malachi 3:10). The practice of tithing has been adapted to Christian service, so we all have a share in spreading the gospel. We can have the satisfaction of knowing we support our pastors and help to make possible all the activities of the church. And everywhere the gospel is preached we know we have a part in it, if we pay our tithes.

The other biblical giving plan is social responsibility. Because in our fallen world some people have more than enough and some are left out, people need us. If we have anything more than what we need, we owe some of it to those less fortunate than we. We feel good when we give because it is something like paying a debt. Caring for the poor is a major part of Christian living. When the crowds asked John the Baptist what they should do to be saved, he told them to repent and then "produce fruit in keeping with repentance." He explained what he meant by telling them to share what they had with the needy (Luke 3:7-11, NIV).

Family Participation

"This is our offering. This is our tithe. We're all in this together."

Begin early to teach young children about tithing. Here is a method that works well with most kids: Let the child hold a dollar bill. Then ask him/her to exchange it with you for 10 dimes. Explain that one dime is the tithe. Have him/her put it into a church offering envelope. Then ask if he/she would like to put another dime into a missions offering. Most children respond eagerly, learn quickly and gain positive ideas about giving.

Writing the check for Sunday's tithes can be an occasion. Express pleasure. Talk about how great it is to have something to share. Explain that the tithe represents the income of the family. Do not try to force children and teen-agers to give from their own gifts and earnings. Rather, set the example and provide a happy environment. Usually they will come to see giving as a privilege rather than a duty and will want to contribute what they can.

A Giving Plan

If you develop a family giving plan, you will find it to be another example of how giving returns many blessings. Nothing does more to strengthen relationships than sharing plans and goals. Family members all gain pleasures and benefits from cooperation, working together to accomplish a purpose, everyone contributing ideas as well as resources. When family focus is turned from personal desires and acquisitions to what we can do for the church and the needy, teen-agers become more aware of others' needs and feelings. You give them opportunities to learn appreciation and habits of caring and giving that will enrich their lives.

When we give material gifts—money, food, clothing—we feel the promised blessing, but another kind of giving brings unique joy. It is giving that involves the giver in a personal, active way. It may or may not require much money, but it always requires something of the giver's being and doing. It is a giving process. I call it "dynamic giving."

I remember being the receiver of a dynamic gift. We were poor migrant workers, a large family huddled together in a leaky tent during an unexpected storm that ruined the harvest season. The welfare agency helped all the migrants with some food and dry bedding. And a church sent a basket. But the best gift came from a family who came through the rain and asked me to come play at their house and eat lunch with them. That was dynamic giving.

You can help your family know the joy of sharing themselves, along with their tithes and offerings. Decide together on special giving projects. Invite a needy family to have a meal with you. Make it a real family meal, with everyone helping in the preparation. On a holiday invite someone to your home who is lonely and left out—an elderly person, a college student, a single adult or someone who has recently moved or suffered a loss.

Offer to care for children or aged persons, so a couple can have an evening together or attend a special church event. Call a local family services agency to find what services may be needed. Volunteer as a family to help at a mission, shelter house, children's home or in an outreach program sponsored by your church. Arrange to visit a home for the elderly. Find out if there is a facility that uses pet therapy where children may take their pets to visit. Being with children and pets is a delightful and healthful experience for many older persons.

"Thank you" will teach more than heavy words of instruction. You can demonstrate that giving is a pleasure by showing appreciation. Probably the greatest mistake in parenting and teaching is the tendency adults have to point out mistakes and give advice. The classic method of positive reinforcement really does work better. Notice unselfish acts of children and teen-agers. Find appropriate ways to ask for their contributions and thank them sincerely. Expressing appreciation to teen-agers may be the best method of keeping them from trouble and helping them to find their life purpose. Those who feel noticed for doing right are more likely to be safe from outside pressures.

Billie Davis, Ed.D., is an educator, sociologist, author and professor emeritus at Evangel University in Springfield, Missouri.

14
KEEPING TEEN-AGERS IN CHURCH

By Jo Ellen Cramer Nicholson

Lesson 1

When I was young, the only time we ever had ice cream was on the way home from church on Sunday nights. What a delight to choose any flavor I wanted. As a child, I started to associate going to church with a very pleasant experience—getting an ice-cream cone.

Years later as a young couple, my husband, Joe, and I continued the practice of positive reinforcement with our children. Not far from our church a hospital had huge fountains with colored lights. On our way home from church we would often take our children to the fountains to let them run around the edges near the sparkling, spraying water. Their squeals of delight disclosed their pleasure and excitement. Other than the frequent visits to the fountain following Sunday evening church services, we rarely did this activity. They also got an ice-cream cone almost every Sunday after church. The form of the positive reinforcement varies as children reach their teens, but remains effective.

Lesson 2

In our family, church attendance was not an option. On Mondays, my dad never asked, "Am I going to work today?" The children never asked, "Am I going to school today?"

Likewise on Sundays, the question, "Are we going to church today?" never came up. It was Sunday; the entire household went to church. If that pattern is established early in life, teen-agers are less likely to question "to go" or "not to go."

Parents should not panic when they hear, "Do I have to go to church today?" It doesn't necessarily mean your child no longer loves the Lord, nor should there be a tirade about the importance of church attendance. Say, "As long as you live at home, we will all attend church together on Sunday." When giving important messages to teen-agers, the fewer words used, the better.

Lesson 3

When driving home after church, do not criticize the service. Finding weaknesses and problems is much easier than coming up with solutions. Nothing ever completely satisfies us as adults. But negative opinions are best kept to oneself; certainly, they should not be expressed in front of children or teen-agers. Young people have difficulty sifting out the good from the bad. If some of it is bad, to them the whole is bad. That is the concrete thinking of children.

Once my daughter said, "Mom, I never know all the bad stuff that goes on at church like some of my friends do." I told her if she ever had a question about what she heard to come to me and I would tell her the truth the best I could.

Lesson 4

Parents, make your home inviting to teen-agers. My husband and I lived just a few miles from church. When we first started looking for a home, we told the real estate agent we must live on the same side of town our church is on. It worked well for our family.

You have only five short years to keep each of your teen-agers in church (ages 13-18). It is so important during these years to keep your home teen friendly. This probably is not the time to buy new carpet or fine furniture. The home needs to be a place where teens will relax and have fun. We often had 50 teen-agers in our small home after Sunday night service. Nothing fancy. Teens love pizza, popcorn or cookies.

Teens also love to be bunched up and crowded. There were spills on the carpet; a favorite rocking chair was broken. Yet, they are joyous memories.

As a youth, I attended a small Assemblies of God church. There was no youth pastor. But a precious, loving adult (Alice May Dye), who taught our teen Sunday school class, had us in her home almost every Friday night for popcorn, games and a devotional.

When the teens are all at your house you never have to worry about where your teens are.

Lesson 5

Youth camps, choir camps and other special camps are an important element of keeping teens in church. After youth camp, many teens report that they were filled with the Holy Spirit and spoke in tongues. These camps are a time for our youth to dedicate themselves more thoroughly to God. Many have been called to specific types of service for our Lord at youth camps. It is during the ages 13-18 that many decide to go to Bible school to become missionaries or ministers.

Lesson 6

The local church shares the responsibility for keeping teen-agers in church. Teen-agers love to be active. They have a deep need to belong to a group. What better group to be identified with than a church youth group?

The local church is strengthened when it offers varied activities for youth. Youth leaders need energy, vigor and intensity coupled with patience and persistence. Some teens who cannot excel at Bible quiz will be superior in a puppet ministry or in musical activities such as handbell choirs, ensembles or instrumental groups. One youth group I know visits a nursing home every Friday night and has a sing-along with the residents. Everyone benefits—nursing home patients, the youth and the church they represent. The nursing home now serves pizza and ice cream after their activity.

Youth activities should be more than just fun and games. Churches need to find creative ways to involve teens in ministry—making sandwiches for the homeless, adopting a grandparent, doing chores for shut-ins. Teens need to learn the joy of giving and doing for others.

Sunday school lessons and youth night sermons should be directed at helping teens face the issues they are dealing with at home and school. Teens need to be taught how to apply the teachings of Jesus. The Bible addresses delicate issues: Homosexuality is sin; sex outside of marriage is wrong; abortion—taking a life—is forbidden; gossip can be worse than murder; criticizing is evil.

Lesson 7

If teens are to remain involved in church, they must feel loved and accepted. Is the atmosphere in your church one where teens may feel they are constantly being criticized by the older generation? To be a teen is to be finding out who you are. Their clothes and hairstyles are ways they have of making a statement of independence. So teens look different from their elders. Yesterday it was long hair and bell-bottom pants. Today it is baggy pants and logo shirts. Tomorrow it may be frayed jeans and shaved heads.

But the eyes remain the same. Look into their eyes as I did last night at church. Those of us over 50 formed a line and had the teens pass in front of us. We were to lay our hands on them and pray for them. When I looked into their faces and their eyes, not much has changed. Many came with tears rolling down their cheeks wanting God's leading. Some came very shyly, eyes downcast, not sure of themselves. Some were almost expressionless. Yet they all came. They wanted to be prayed for; they welcomed a hug; they needed to be accepted and appreciated.

The challenge to the current adult generation is to make

our churches a place where a teen—any teen (even with green hair, earrings, baggy pants)—will feel the love of Jesus Christ. Not all homes are loving, safe places. The way to keep today's teen in church is to fill it with love. Teens recognize the real thing. Money spent on pizza, pop and ice cream is well invested. Then teach them, involve them. Utilize their talents in worship, in ministry, in outreach. Help them to associate the church with pleasant times where they are taught how to live in today's world.

Teen involvement in church means parent involvement in church. Every activity mentioned takes volunteer time. One person cannot conduct all of these activities; it takes a whole team. None of these teen activities just happens. They take time, effort and planning.

Soon, should the Lord tarry, today's teens will be our youth pastors, our pastors and our church leaders.

Pray for the teen-agers you know. Ask the Lord to build a wall of protection about them. Ask Him to guide them in every activity. Prayer changes things; prayer changes teens.

Jo Ellen Cramer Nicholson is a retired nurse. She lives in Springfield, Missouri.

15
HOW TO BE A GREAT DAD

By Del Guynes

What makes a father a really great dad? Here are 10 factors that contribute significantly.

Great dads pray for and before their kids. Praying "before" their kids does not mean being the first in a sequence; it means praying "in front" of them. It's easier to pray in public if one is regular about praying in private. I'm convinced that dads get intense spiritual opposition when they demonstrate spiritual leadership before others, especially members of their own families. It comes in different forms, but the one I'm most familiar with is a reticence to initiate "spiritual activity" in situations outside of the normal religious zones such as church and saying grace before meals.

For example, do you ever hesitate to initiate a spontaneous prayer circle when sad news comes? I do. To be great dads, we need to step into the praying-in-front-of-your-kids spot.

Great dads let their kids in on God's leading. Sometimes a great dad has to keep decision-making between him and Mom. Uncertainty about location and established relationships can bring stress to children. However, there are times when spiritual growth will come to our kids when they can be a part of either a current decision being made or how a previous decision was made.

Recently, the Lord spoke quite clearly to our oldest child through the Scriptures, confirming a decision we were making. Another child was excited about hearing how God was going to do what He had spoken to us, even though we didn't have the answer at the time. Our concern was that the uncertainty might burden her, until we saw the excitement in her eyes.

Great dads include their children in their decision-making, which will lay a foundation for their own decision-making throughout their lives.

Great dads let their kids see their concern for the lost. Often it's easier to be concerned for the lost at large, especially if they live out of town or out of the country. Sometimes it's not as easy to show concern for the lost person next door.

Great dads tell their kids the stories of when they've shared the gospel with an unbelieving friend. It helps kids to see that not all sowing brings an opportunity to reap. They will be encouraged to be sowers, regardless of the results.

Great dads pray with their children for schoolmates, business associates and neighbors so they will see the gospel as relevant in every area.

Great dads make travel count. A traveling dad's professional commitments are perhaps the most likely external factors to place stress on his family. Traveling can be a tremendous burden on a dad wanting to excel both in the workplace and at home. Great dads will evaluate whether they really have to stay out of town that extra half day and sometimes they'll have the family meet them upon arrival to go out for dinner.

Great dads occasionally give each child special treatment. Great dads find ways to let each child feel special. They take their kids out to eat—one at a time. Great dads let their children join them at work—one at a time. Great dads let each child in on a special secret. Of course, great care must be taken to avoid imbalance. These activities reinforce the uniqueness of each child.

Great dads custom design every discipline. Great dads concentrate on the appropriate response to behavior problems. They don't dispose of a discipline matter with a standard approach, when the particulars call for a customized approach.

Great dads are great husbands. Someone said, "To be a great dad, you first have to be a great husband." Great dads demonstrate greatness in their relationships with their wives. Our kids derive benefits from Mom and Dad's relationship— especially a sense of security.

I've found if there's strife among our children, it often is due to underlying tension between their mom and me. I saw a T-shirt that said, "When Momma's not happy, ain't nobody happy." Great dads keep Momma happy.

Focusing on one's marriage helps prevent children from being used as surrogates to meet spouses' needs for affection and affirmation.

Great dads are sensitive to cross-gender affinity. Great dads aren't afraid to physically demonstrate affection for their daughters. They don't allow society's alarm about child abuse to diminish the manner in which they demonstrate tenderness and affection. At the same time, they are wise about how best to do so based on their daughter's maturity level.

Great dads continue to be great dads throughout their lives. As an adult, I am still being shaped by my dad's input. I'm thankful for what he was to me when I was in his house, and it hasn't stopped just because I moved out of the house. I still need my father's example, and I recognize that my kids will need my example when they have homes of their own.

Great dads have meaningful relationships with their children throughout their lives.

Great dads do what they know to do. When I told my four kids that I was writing about being a great dad, they laughed. In that lighthearted moment I told them that many of us dads probably know how to be great dads, but we don't always do the great-dad stuff.

To be sure, there are clever and creative ideas that we can glean from one another that might make us more effective, but the Lord has arranged it so that there is no one better qualified to be dad to your kids than you are. He has promised to provide the wisdom, grace, insight, firmness and affection your kids need from you. In other words, God gives you the resources you need to be a great dad, so "just do it."

Let's risk getting out of some of our comfort zones and be the great dads our kids deserve.

Del Guynes is minister of music at First Assembly of God in Aurora, Colorado.

16

CLAIMING YOUR CHILDREN FOR CHRIST

By Charles S. Price

The blinds were down in the home of Grandma Simmons. I was feeling very tired and chilly as I stepped out of the car to go to the little home where an angel was waiting to carry a soul through the portals to eternal rest. The driving rain on the windshield had made travel very slow, and I had time to think and pray over the words that would bring comfort in such an hour.

Gently I knocked at the door.

What a contrast the interior of that little home presented to the cold and rain outside. In one corner two people were kneeling in prayer; others stood around a bed that was wreathed with the glory of the Lord and gently patted a thin, wrinkled hand. Little did I realize that Grandma Simmons was going to settle a question in my heart that had never been answered.

The dear saint was still conscious. There were moments when her mind seemed to wander, but some words of comfort from the people who loved her seemed to bring the tangled threads together, and she was able to talk coherently, her voice scarcely above a whisper. All her children were there; however, all were not saved.

As I took her wrinkled hand in mine, there was an

atmosphere of comfort and warmth even in the presence of death. Her children loved her dearly. They knew that probably before the break of another day she would be at home with Jesus. There was the sorrow of parting, but also the joy of meeting again. She looked into the faces of her children and said softly: "My children, I know I shall meet you all there. My Lord has given me His promise."

Parental Role

How can a Christian parent be happy in the contemplation that some of his/her children are lost? If Jesus could weep with compassion over the lost of Jerusalem, it is inconceivable that He should expect us to climb the mountain peaks of glory and rejoice with our heads above the clouds when those we love are wandering in the dark, deep valleys of sin below.

Because a mother is saved, does that mean that every member of the family is saved as well? If the father confesses Christ as his Savior, does it mean that on the virtue of that confession alone all of the children are covered with the blood of Christ? No!

In God's redemption plan, it is imperative for every individual to accept the blood that was shed on Calvary as atonement for sin. Men and women cannot be saved by proxy; they must decide the question of their soul's salvation for themselves. I believe there are many Spirit-filled and Blood-washed Christians whose children have died in sin and will never see the inside of the gates of pearl. If these things then be true, what becomes of the promise of Acts 16:31*, "Believe on the Lord Jesus Christ, and thou shalt be saved, and thy house"?

In sincerity and faith in Jesus we must commit our loved ones to His care and keep interceding for them. Perhaps the day will come when they will surrender their hearts to Him only after Mother has gone to glory. Perhaps it will be after

*All Scripture references in this chapter are from the King James Version.

Father has been laid away. But that does not alter the parents' responsibility to lift them up in prayer. You must commit your loved ones to Jesus and in faith and in confidence trust that the day will come when the convicting power of the Holy Spirit will be so great they will not be able to resist. Claim their souls for God and never give up.

I want to encourage all of you who have sons and daughters out of the ark of safety. Do not relax in your vigilance in talking to them about Jesus. Do not forget the necessity of prayer. But how great the joy and how wonderful the peace that comes when we hold our children up before the Lord and claim for them the Kingdom.

What Paul said to the jailer the night he was delivered by the power of the Lord from the prison at Philippi (Acts 16:31, above) showed the importance of faith—on the part of everyone who would be saved. Belief started with the jailer, who passed that faith along to his household. He could not believe for them, but he could influence them to have faith. They all did; and they were all saved.

Sam Jones

Sam Jones' father was dying in Georgia. The village was Sam's hometown, Cartersville. Sam had gone deep into sin and had become a drunkard. He had lost his law practice and what money he possessed slipped through his fingers as he walked the broad highway of self-indulgence.

When the doctor told his father there was no hope, he called his wife to his side and said: "My dear, I want you to go downtown after Sam."

Soon Sam was by the bed of his dying father. Years before the Lord had promised him that one day Sam would be brought into the fold. He told his son that it would add to his cup of happiness if he could see with his own eyes that glorious event. Sam broke. Kneeling by his father's bedside he found Christ as Savior.

The Spirit of the Lord rested upon that new convert as he preached the gospel. Some of the cities in America were shaken by the convicting power of the Holy Spirit, and thousands found Christ as personal Savior through his ministry.

Mother, claim your children for God. Father, plead for the salvation of your household. Parents, show your family Jesus. "Train up a child in the way he should go: and when he is old, he will not depart from it" (Proverbs 22:6). Just like the family of the Philippian jailer, the decision must be theirs: "He . . . rejoiced, believing in God with all his house" (Acts 16:34). But parents can play the strongest role in the ultimate decision of their household. There is no higher intercession or more forceful spiritual warfare than the prayerful wrestling of a parent for his or her child.

Remember that intercession, faith and influence have power in bringing salvation. Do not relax; continue faithfully asking the Lord to save your children, and believe that He will do it.

Charles S. Price (1887-1947) was a Pentecostal evangelist, pastor and teacher. This chapter was updated and abridged from an article published in the March 29, 1947, *Pentecostal Evangel.*

RELATIONSHIPS

"Be kind and compassionate to
one another."

— Ephesians 4:32 (NIV)

17
RESPECT FOR MOM

By T. Ray Rachels

A woman in a van passed me in the fast lane, hauling four kids, all under 13. As she went by, I noticed her license-plate holder: "Need a taxi? Call 1-800-MOM."
There's nobody like Mom. The whole world may go out, but she always comes in. And it's easy to take her for granted.

For instance, I read a *Wall Street Journal* report on three-time mother Michelle Tribout of Belleville, Illinois.

It began when a reporter from the town's *News-Democrat* walked by the Tribout house and spotted Michelle in a tree house. She was telling her husband, on the ground below, that she wasn't coming down or cooking or cleaning until the kids started pitching in and showing some gratitude.

Next morning, after the *News-Democrat* published a photo of her sitting in the tree house, crews from five TV stations showed up, along with a reporter from *People* magazine. The British Broadcasting Corporation called, as did a radio station representative from Australia.

It seems the children—Misty, 15; Joseph, 13; and Rachel, 7—had been fighting, talking back and failing to get out of bed, Tribout said. The final straw came when they missed a pancake breakfast, even after she made five trips upstairs to wake them.

When the children came home from school that afternoon, they found their mom in the tree house and a big note on

91

the mailbox. It read: "On strike Mom. No cooking, cleaning, doctoring, banking or taxi service. Out of order."

Her husband, Sonny, an appliance repairman, supported the strike. So the kids cooked dinner and came outside promising to be nice. But Tribout didn't budge. "I was shocked," says Joseph. "I thought she would be up there for days."

Next, the children baked their mom's favorite brownies and wrote up a settlement promising to:

1. Pitch in whenever you see something needs to be done.
2. Act your age, not like you are 5.
3. Don't smart off.
4. Come when you are called.
5. We are the kids; you are the parents.
6. Give and take on an equal basis.
7. Ask before you do something.
8. Do not hit or hurt anybody.

They presented the settlement at 11:30 p.m. A contract was reached at midnight, and Tribout came down.

She was a wit's-end mom who, with serious humor, negotiated her way through some of the frustrations of motherhood and showed how tough daily living can get.

Sons and daughters, remember:

She's Mom. Respect and honor her as the closest gift to heaven God has given you on earth.

She's Mom. Give your personal best to every effort at holding up a standard of excellence at home and in your community, making her proud of you.

She's Mom. Honesty and truth-telling will build her trust and confidence in you and make you an honored person.

She's Mom. Responsibility begins at home for you with the smallest tasks and will lift burdens and loads from her shoulders.

She's Mom. Compassion and a gentle way will extend joy and comfort through the years and make her heart lighter.

She's Mom. Self-discipline will keep her from saying something to you again and again and will strengthen your will for choosing wisely.

She's Mom. Perseverance and steadfastness are qualities in you she needs to count on for the times when quitting would be the easiest way out.

She's Mom. Give to her and then give some more. Relationships grow best when giving is more generously done than taking.

She's Mom. Don't take her for granted.

T. Ray Rachels is superintendent of the Southern California District of the Assemblies of God.

18

UNDERSTANDING TEEN-AGERS

By John Benton

t's scary raising teen-agers. You don't know what they're going to do next.

Some even try suicide—and succeed.

Suicide usually happens between the ages of 17 and 19. Why would young people commit suicide when they have their whole lives ahead of them?

One basic cause is frustration. Kids are frustrated about their past, their present and their future.

Here are some things that really frustrate teen-agers:

They feel pressure to be successful. Our society puts pressure on all of us to be successful. No one loves a failure.

Our teen-agers receive their SAT scores. They discuss the scores among themselves, and nobody wants to look bad. Out of frustration over their inability to handle schoolwork, some teen-agers think the answer is to kill themselves.

They are frustrated because we judge by what we get, not what we give. We live in an "I want" society, not an "I'll give" society. This desire for material goods frustrates some teen-agers—especially those from lower-income homes. Even in our churches, material success is often equated with spirituality, and this confuses teens.

Materialism becomes an obsession. Better cars, better clothes, and better homes—these goals are confusing to a teen who tries to understand the simple lifestyle Jesus taught.

They experience a letdown after they graduate. School can be very intense—especially the senior year when they're trying to cram it all in. And after school is out, there's a lot of unscheduled time for teen-agers to deal with. Boredom becomes a difficult obstacle to overcome.

They have an unknown future. It's difficult for them to decide what they want to be. Job opportunities today are so varied.

When I was growing up, kids talked about being a fireman, policeman or doctor. Today you name it, and you can probably become one. That's why it's difficult for teen-agers to decide who they really want to be or what they should be doing.

They are frustrated because they can't break bad habits. A young woman who had been in and out of our rehabilitation program left for the last time. She would never stay long enough to get her life straightened out. As soon as she would encounter something difficult, she would leave. That was her way of dealing with her frustrations.

This last time she left, she was picked up by the police. In a jail cell she took her blouse and hanged herself.

We were devastated, but we also knew this girl's frustration at not being able to break her drug habit.

Teens not only face habits of drug addiction but other frustrations—weight, promiscuity, pornography, smoking, bulimia, anorexia.

Now let me share how you can help your teens get rid of some of these frustrations.

Define success. There are many definitions of success, but the one I like best is, "Success is discovering God's will for your life."

This has to do with the talents God has given us. Jesus talked about the person with five talents, the one with two talents, and the one with only one. (See Matthew 25:14-30.) When they used their talents successfully, there were great rewards. When they weren't used, there was punishment.

Sit with your teens and pray with them concerning the talents God has given them. Then help them discover what they should be doing in life.

Success has also been defined as a journey. It is not a destination, and teens need to know that.

Success is never measured by what we have, what we accomplish or even by how popular we are.

Let them know that some of the most successful people in the world are not wealthy or well-known. But in the eyes of God they are successful because they have fulfilled His will for their lives.

Teach what the Bible says: "It is more blessed to give than to receive" (Acts 20:35, KJV). Set the example. Are you a giving person? If you're not, start with yourself. Whether you like it or not, you teach by example.

Giving is not only monetary; it also means giving our time. Look for opportunities to give.

That may mean inviting someone who needs a meal over for supper. Maybe it means running an errand. Encourage your teens to open their hearts to someone in need. Then work with them to satisfy that need.

Don't let the doldrums set in after they get out of high school. Begin to plan activities before they get out of school.

Try to line up a job for them. If you can, take some of your vacation in the spring so you can help them plan for that summer job. Possibly they can work in a church camp. Or if there is a transition time between high school and college, they may want to volunteer at some charitable organization.

Don't let the future be unknown. Teach them to put their trust in God. Become filled with a sense of expectancy. Believe God for the miraculous. Challenge the future with your faith in God, and allow your teen-agers the privilege of exercising faith with you.

Teach them to replace a bad habit with a good habit.

My desire to get up early and pray for an hour every morning taught me a great lesson about developing good habits. I am not an early morning person, so I knew it was going to be hard. But I also knew it had to be done if I was to be effective.

Replacing a bad habit with a good one sounds simple, doesn't it? I learned three keys: desire, discipline and delight.

First, desire. I really felt I should pray that hour—I desired it.

We all desire things. In my case it was a closer walk with God. It could be to lose weight, to give up drugs—whatever.

The next step, discipline. There was the discipline of getting up earlier to have that time with God. I had to force myself to get up. But I knew I had to do this.

Now I spend an hour and a half or longer with the Lord each morning. Because I made this great discovery, I have delight.

Here's a suggestion. Have your teen-agers read this chapter. Then ask them to talk it over with you. And listen to them. This will be a wonderful opportunity for a meaningful discussion.

Be honest and open, and you'll help your teen-ager develop into the person God desires him/her to be.

John Benton, an Assemblies of God minister, is president and founder of the Walter Hoving Home in Garrison, New York.

19
WHAT MAKES AN EFFECTIVE GRANDPARENT?

By Raymond T. Brock

One of God's special gifts to aging adults is the privilege of becoming grandparents. Having weathered the storms of childhood and adolescence with their own children, parents of adult children have been exposed to the joys and sorrows that come with guiding young lives into adulthood. Lessons learned in the process form the curriculum grandparents draw upon to add a special dimension to the lives of the children of their children that can only come from age, experience and maturity.

When my wife and I celebrated our 50th wedding anniversary recently, one of the joys of the reception was to see our grandchildren participating in the festivities with friends we had accumulated through the years. The eagerness of these pre-teens to be helpful brought a new appreciation for what young lives can contribute to the multigenerational family. Effective grandparents can take humble pride in being available to the children of their children in the ordinary events of their lives as well as the crises and triumphs.

What contributions can grandparents give to their grandchildren? Let's look at them in the form of gifts.

Availability. Just being there is a primary ingredient of being an effective grandparent. Too many times the busyness of life plagues contemporary families. With both parents working out of the home, with one parent working more than one job, with children coming home to an empty house as latchkey children, many find themselves standing on the sidelines watching life passing them by. They need grandparents to be available with time and attention. This is more than baby-sitting. It is sharing their joys and sorrows. It is caring about sibling rivalries, homework, hobbies, recreations and friends.

Involvement. Children need grandparents to be involved with them. Grandmothers have a special place in the lives of their grandchildren when they are included in the everyday tasks of living. Making beds, cooking, sewing, cleaning, doing the laundry and ironing are among the tasks children need to learn under unpressured conditions which their own homes frequently lack.

Grandfathers are needed to explain and demonstrate the arts of maintaining a house, taking care of a car and caring for the yard.

Information. This is the "how to do it" contribution of grandparents that only seasoned adults can give. Having traversed the first half of their lives, grandparents have accumulated innumerable skills, both vocational and avocational, that can enrich the lives of the younger generation. This is especially true in hobbies and crafts as well as leisure-time activities. Research has demonstrated that adults seldom enjoy in retirement hobbies and recreations they were not at least exposed to or in which they did not experiment in their younger years. Introducing such leisure time activities, beyond the contact sports and physically exhausting physical challenges, will enhance the lives of the offspring not only in childhood and youth, but in their own mature years.

Experience. The younger set has an insatiable curiosity about what life was like in the "good old days." I remember sitting in my grandfather's lap listening to what life was like in the Civil War era, when his brothers went off to fight for their convictions—half for the North and half for the South. Grandmother talked about what it was like when the "bushwhackers" came marauding through the country-side while the men were off to war.

My own children hung on to every word my father would divulge about his youth, especially his courtship days "squir-ing" my mother in a "surrey with a fringe on top."

Now, when I reflect on my ministry, travels and people I have met, my grandchildren are wide-eyed and attentive. Recalling the drama of the ages links the past with the pres-ent and sparks eager anticipation for what is yet to come, as Jesus tarries.

Wisdom. King David wrote, "The fear of the Lord is the beginning of wisdom" (Psalm 111:10*). Imparting spiritual wisdom to grandchildren is a privilege as well as a responsi-bility. The example of consistent Christian living is priceless. Let your grandchildren see you reading the Bible. Tell them what God's Word means to you. Let them hear you pray, not only at the table over meals, but in family and personal devotions. Talk to them about your faith and how it has sus-tained you in the trying times of life. Share with them your spiritual struggles and your victories. Be honest with them about how you handled the temptations of life and discov-ered the abiding presence of the Lord in your daily walk (Romans 8:38,39).

Example. The most effective way to influence young lives is by example. This "life without words" illustrates to grand-children what it means to have a value system anchored in Christ. One writer has observed, "What you are speaks so loudly I can't hear what you say." Many a young person has been won to Christ because of the example of a grandparent who lived a consistent testimony.

Listening. Contemporary life is short on listening skills. One of the greatest contributions grandparents can make to the lives of their grandchildren is to listen to them when they trust enough to bare their hearts. They only share their inmost thoughts to someone who has demonstrated a desire to listen.

*All Scripture references in this chapter are from the King James Version.

When you listen, you don't interrupt. You don't ask questions. You don't probe for information. When you listen, you give undivided attention. You maintain eye contact and, if possible, physical touch. Your focused attention attests to your love for the child and your eagerness to be a part of his or her life. Attentive listening often affords the opportunity to make a specific input into the life of your grandchild that otherwise would not be welcomed.

Guidance. Guidance is not telling. It is not criticism. It is not condemning. Guidance is taking a life situation your grandchild has shared with you and examining how it could be handled in a more creative or constructive way. It is looking for new ways to handle old problems. It is offering biblical solutions to contemporary problems and spiritual ways of looking at life's challenges, paradoxes and inconsistencies. We have to admit that life is not fair, but God is always good. Ultimately, "all things work together for good to them that love God, to them who are the called according to his purpose" (Romans 8:28).

Faith. There is no greater gift grandparents can give their grandchildren than a faith to live by (Habakkuk 2:4). But, more important, it is a faith to die by. Coming to the close of life with a dignity that has been spawned by a life of integrity is the ultimate contribution of grandparents to their grandchildren. The value of this gift will carry over into the afterlife when extended families gather in eternity together. May God grant that your family and mine will be an unbroken circle around the Throne of God.

We have looked at nine gifts effective grandparents give to their grandchildren. Let us consider these as our legacy for our grandchildren to inherit—gifts that bear fruit.

Raymond T. Brock, Ed.D., an Assemblies of God minister, is a licensed counselor.

20
CARING FOR AN AGING PARENT

By Marlene Bagnull

I awoke instantly at the first ring.

"I'm confused," my mother said, her voice shaky. "I'm supposed to be getting the bus for school, but they're not answering the phone. I don't know what I should do."

"You don't have to do anything but go back to bed, Mother," I said. "It's 4 in the morning."

My mother has a dementia similar to Alzheimer's. Confusion was her frequent companion, just as worry had become mine.

Did I make the right decision to move her out of her home into an apartment? Was I providing adequate support? Once someone found her wandering around the apartment complex. What if something had happened to her?

Suppose something happened to me—to my health, to my family? Could we bear the stress Mom's care was placing on our lives? How long would it be before we reached our breaking point—before we were forced to put Mom in a home? And then how would we cope with her anger and hurt?

When my stepfather died, I knew Mom would have to move East. No one back home could assume responsibility for her, and we certainly could not monitor her care from 800 miles away. When I finally convinced her to come for a "visit," I knew she wouldn't be returning home. But I really didn't know how bad she was or how time-consuming her care would be.

The hospital I admitted her to for assessment didn't give us a hopeful prognosis. Tests showed "serious and irreversible organic brain dysfunction." Mom wasn't going to get better. And it was just a matter of time until she got worse.

The doctor recommended placement in a personal care home. I visited half a dozen and prayed for guidance. I knew it would be the easiest way, perhaps even the best for Mom. But I didn't have peace about placing her in one.

There was no way Mom could live with us. We didn't have room. The alternative seemed to be an apartment.

I talked with a geriatric planning counselor and sought advice from friends. Everyone agreed I should give it a try. And God appeared to be blessing my plans when a first-floor apartment in the building next to my married daughter became available.

Mom was delighted with her new home. She walked around the apartment patting furniture she hadn't seen in two months. I knew we had done the right thing.

The first few days Mom was great. My daughter checked on her frequently. She monitored Mom's meals and medicine and made sure Mom was waiting each morning for the van from the senior center. We all rejoiced in how well Mom was adjusting.

I should have realized it wouldn't be that easy, but we believe what we want to believe. Therefore, I wasn't prepared for the phone calls I began getting all hours of the day and night. Mom was confused and disoriented and very belligerent when we didn't drop everything and make her the center of our attention.

I wanted to run away. But where? There was no escaping the demands Mom made upon me or the guilt I felt when I wasn't spending time with her. Unable to cope, I turned to the Lord. The principles He taught me will help you if you are caring for an aging parent.

1. *Don't allow yourself to be consumed by your loved one's needs or demands.* No matter how much I did for Mom or

how much time I spent with her, it would never be enough. The Lord helped me know I could not allow her to manipulate me or make me feel guilty. It is not only OK to set limits and be firm, it is essential.

2. *Resist trying to squeeze 30 hours into 24.* No matter how many hours we have, there will never be enough. We need to learn how to better use the hours God does give us. Learn to bring balance to each 24 hours by taking time for rest and recreation. To drive ourselves to do more and more will compound the problem if we end up folding.

3. *Contract out what others can do to reserve your time and energy for what you alone can give—your love.* This freed me to employ others to do tasks that did not have to be done by me. Not only did it take some of the pressure off me, it gave Mom contact with others and the advantage of their expertise.

4. *Refuse to nurse fearful thoughts about your own aging.* The enemy can torture us with the fear that we'll end up the same way when we watch our mother or father's health deteriorating. But as a friend reminded me, "I'm a new creation. I have new genes!"

5. *No matter how bleak things look, remember "there are three things that remain—faith, hope, and love"* (1 Corinthians 13:13, *Living Bible*). God promises to remain faithful even when I am too weak to have any faith left. (See 2 Timothy 2:13.) He also promises that no one who hopes in Him will ever be put to shame. (See Psalm 25:3.) His love will enable me to go through and grow through the problems of caring for my mother. In His strength I can love her when she is unlovable. And in His strength I'll also be able to love her enough to do what I have to do, even if that someday means putting her in a home. I can trust Him a day at a time knowing He will not fail her or me.

Marlene Bagnull, an author and writers conference director, lives in Drexel Hill, Pennsylvania.

21
REACHING UNSAVED LOVED ONES

By Michael H. Clarensau

He's standing! The sudden surge of joy caught me off-guard. Tears charted their own course as the remarkable scene made a deep imprint on my soul. *My grandfather is standing—standing to receive Christ as his Savior.*

The morning had started like many previous Sundays. A few dozen people filed into the sanctuary, taking their customary places as the Sunday school teacher prepared to assume the small podium. I glanced around, meeting pleasant smiles, my role as guest speaker growing evident. My wife and two sons sat beside me, hoping our invitation might receive a surprising response.

It did. Class announcements had just begun when two forms appeared in the doorway. My wife squeezed my hand as we shared a silent celebration—my grandparents had come.

I watched with disguised delight as the pastor led them toward our front pew. Curious but friendly glances came from around the room as these "visitors" settled into the conspicuous seating.

Some 20 years had passed since my grandmother received Christ. It had been my mother's joy to lead her mother to the Lord.

My grandfather settled uncomfortably in the pew. This was not his arena. Through his 79 years, churches had been for weddings, funerals and other necessary occasions. I marveled that he would risk such discomfort just to hear his grandson preach.

An hour later I joined the pastor on the platform for the time of worship. I smiled as my boys adjusted their seating so each could nestle against their great-grandfather. Somehow they seemed to understand this moment's significance. For more than 30 years my mother had prayed for her father.

I finished the message and extended the opportunity for all to know the Christ I had preached.

That's when it happened. I lifted my eyes to scan the crowd when I saw him. My grandfather was standing. Pews that had rarely held him held him no longer. Flanked by two smiling boys, he looked at me with eyes that blended determination and desperation. My wife hugged my grandmother as they realized the event. I shook myself from the stunning scene and led him in the sinner's prayer. My oldest son leaned close to his great-grandfather, listening intently. I rejoiced, anticipating the opportunity to call my mother and tell her that her most urgent prayers had been answered. My grandfather had received Christ.

Nearly every Christian comprehends the pain of friends or family members away from God. Few congregational prayers omit the yearning for unsaved loved ones. Some call the names of children raised with God's Word but living by a different path. Others plead for a spouse who cares little for God. Still others name friends who need Christ and cringe at the thought of spending eternity apart from them.

Many scan the Scriptures in search of a promise or guarantee of the answer they seek. Others diligently copy passages they will share at the right opportunity. Somehow, some way, victory must be achieved.

We all want the experience of the nobleman in John 4:53. His encounter with Christ's power caused his entire family to be saved. And, what joy must have filled Lydia's heart at the salvation of her household (Acts 16:15). Many of us would stand with the Philippian jailer at the point of death to know his joy of watching his entire household accept Christ (Acts 16:33). If it were up to us, we would surely join Joshua in proclaiming the allegiance of our entire family to God (Joshua 24:15). Still, some of our lambs remain far from the fold.

How does the Bible counsel us on this critical issue? Certainly we will not find a one-size-fits-all strategy for such evangelism. Yet, our concerns were far from foreign to many Bible characters. Somewhere in the midst of their experiences and teachings we can find guidance and hope.

Step 1: *Pray.* Every hunger for spiritual blessing must have prayer at its core. Boundaries melt away when we communicate with the One who knows no limitations.

The Bible teaches us that the key to successful prayer is our connection to the will of God. The leper's cry, "If it be your will," moved the Savior (Mark 1:40). How marvelous to realize that the will of God for the unsaved is clearly carved for all to see: He is "not willing that any should perish, but that all should come to repentance" (2 Peter 3:9, KJV). How wonderful to know that the desire of your heart matches the desire of God.

To most of us, Job is the man who lifted his voice to God though his body was ravaged by boils. But, in Job 1:5, he can be seen at the altar before God, offering sacrifices to sanctify his children. We, too, must faithfully call to the One who saves.

Step 2: *Witness.* This word captures the essence of biblical evangelism. Witnessing is not theological salesmanship. It is not the ability to define your beliefs and share them with others. To witness is to tell others what you've experienced.

Jesus healed a demon-possessed man and told him to go and tell his family what God had done for him (Luke 8:39). The woman at the well did the same after her encounter with the One who "told me everything I ever did" (John 4:29, NIV). Jesus' parting command (Acts 1:8) calls us to do the same—be witnesses.

Most of us know the sad result of trying to tell our loved ones how to live. Our efforts to impose our beliefs are usually met with an unscalable wall of resistance. But a testimony of what God has done in our lives can't be refuted. An uneducated blind man silenced the most cynical scoffers with the words, "I was blind but now I see!" (John 9:25, NIV).

Step 3: *Love*. It is not our ability to live flawlessly that draws people to God, but our ability to love. Everyone wants to stop and be around someone who loves. Paul told us this love has been poured into our hearts (Romans 5:5), while John claims it to be the distinguishing mark of Christ in us (1 John 4:7).

Saul of Tarsus was a man who could only be moved by love. Stephen's love moved him. Stephen's words caused Saul to help stone him. Stephen's love and forgiveness landed a crushing blow to Saul's heart. Later, it was Saul, now Paul, who prayed that God would help him give his life with such love (Philippians 1:20).

Step 4: *Wait*. The experience we desire for our loved ones is one of revolutionary life change. Premature commitments born of our impatience will only bring greater heartache. Like the Prodigal's father, we must wait for the one we love to "come to his senses" (Luke 15:17).

Each of us must face crisis in order to willingly abandon the old life for the new. While this may be the most painful of moments, heaven will be filled with those who turned to Christ in the midst of agony.

The final step: *Trust*. How marvelous to know that the Maker of life is on our side in this issue. God has repeatedly proved himself as capable of our "impossibles." Trust Him. Do not let go of the hope that is in you, for He is the God who saves.

Michael H. Clarensau is editor in chief of the Sunday School Curriculum and Literature Department at the Assemblies of God Headquarters.

22
LIFE AFTER BETRAYAL

By Ruth Hetzendorfer

As the door slammed, I knew my husband had walked out for the last time. I ran to my bedroom, sobbing uncontrollably. My 5-year-old daughter quietly walked in and crawled on my bed where I was lying. She brushed her hand across my head with short strokes saying, "It'll be all right, Mommy."

No words could express the feeling I had when my entire life and dreams were ripped out from under me. I felt my life was over and that there was no hope.

During this time of shock and confusion, I found myself constantly examining what I could have done to make things different. I truly did not know what had happened. One day my life appeared intact; the next day, I had been exchanged for someone else.

Every day was a struggle. It seemed that everything in the house was constantly breaking. Even caring for my children's immediate needs seemed overwhelming. I felt afraid and was also very angry at life, at God and particularly at my husband.

Each morning for one year, I woke up immediately thinking, *How could this have happened to me?* Then the tears would start all over again. Somehow I knew we would all find a way to survive, but the most difficult thought was that somehow I had failed God. I had dreamed of being in

111

ministry since I was 8 years old. I had patterned my life after my mother, saying that someday I would be married to an anointed man of God and have an effective ministry. Now it seemed my dreams were over.

The financial aspect of taking care of a family was just a small part of the overwhelming cares that impacted my life. I found it difficult to be the father and mother I felt my children needed. My parents and sister were halfway around the world serving as missionaries. My church didn't know what to do for me. I felt abandoned and alone.

During this time I had enmeshed myself in fasting, praying and searching the Scriptures. On one of those days while I was preparing for a day of teaching school, I felt an overpowering sense of hopelessness. The Lord led me to Jeremiah 30:16,17*: " 'But all who devour you will be devoured . . . I will restore you to health and heal your wounds,' declares the Lord, 'because you are called an outcast, Zion for whom no one cares.' "

If God made me, then He could heal me. If His promises were true, they were true for me too. I had mourned for a year. I decided that was enough. I realized that Satan had deceived me into thinking I was worth nothing because of one man's rejection of me. I claimed Genesis 50:20: "You intended to harm me, but God intended it for good to accomplish what is now being done, the saving of many lives." I wrote it out and placed it on my wall. It was a beginning.

Thirteen years have passed. Soon my daughters will be graduating from a Christian university. They love the Lord, have effective prayer lives and exhibit the attributes of maturity and emotional health. I am counseling the hurting and teaching others how to counsel at the same university. My dreams for ministry have come true. We have no doubt that God has used what was meant for evil, for our good. How did our lives change?

---

*All Scripture references in this chapter are from the New International Version.

The following describes what God taught me. What He has done for me, He will do for you.

1. *Bless your enemies.* "Do not repay anyone evil for evil . . . live at peace with everyone. Do not take revenge, my friends, but leave room for God's wrath, for it is written, 'It is mine to avenge; I will repay,' says the Lord. On the contrary: 'If your enemy is hungry, feed him' . . . overcome evil with good" (Romans 12:17-21).

During the first year that my husband left, the Lord gave me this Scripture. I realized that God was telling me that I was responsible for my attitude toward the situation. I also knew that I would be of no use to my children unless I had something from within to give them. James 3:3-16 tells us that in order to be wise and to prosper, we have to do what God asks of us in all humility.

I started asking the Lord to bless my husband and his girl-friend. Who could be more of an enemy than a woman who had been previously engaged to my husband? This was "the one" he had told me about during our first year of marriage, saying that he "would always have a quirk for her." I chose to take my hands off them and let God take charge. The words often stuck in my mouth and I didn't feel what I was saying, but I did it as an act of my will—I asked the Lord to bless them.

2. *Forgive those who sin against you.* " 'Lord, how many times shall I forgive my brother when he sins against me? Up to seven times?' Jesus answered, 'I tell you, not seven times, but seventy-seven times' " (Matthew 18:21,22).

At this point, the Lord was bringing me to a place of for-giveness. In this type of situation it is easy to allow a "root of bitterness" to grow (Hebrews 12:14,15). Bitterness evolves by reacting out of personal hurt. It produces fruit such as anger, resentment and evil speaking. Those fruits were in my life. Because I knew the importance of forgiving, I had to start asking God to "help me to choose to forgive" (Matthew 18:23-27). It wasn't just my husband or his girlfriend I had anger toward; it was God. How could God let me marry my husband when He knew what would happen 12 years later? I had fasted three days before deciding to marry. I had even gone back to God again to reaffirm what He had spoken. Why didn't God speak to me then?

I came to peace with God when I came to the only recognition that I could: God gives man and woman free choice. He will deal, He will convict, but He will not change a person's will. He gives us the road to follow, but we must choose if we really do believe that God is good. Do we believe the promises in His Word are for us?

3. *Praise God in all things.* "Give thanks to the Lord Almighty, for the Lord is good; his love endures forever. 'For I will restore the fortunes of the land as they were before,' says the Lord" (Jeremiah 33:11). Job 5:22 says, "You will laugh at destruction and famine, and need not fear the beasts of the earth." Isaiah 61:1-3 describes how God will give the brokenhearted a spirit of praise instead of a spirit of despair.

One cannot be defeated or discouraged when he or she is continually giving praise to God. Being in the midst of divorce does not naturally bring laughter. I had to recognize that praising God "in all things" was demonstrating to God that I trusted Him in all things (Ephesians 5:20). Praise releases power to work in the situation for good.

I discovered that praise began with my life as it was at the moment. I looked up all the Scriptures on praise and studied how God used praisers to win the battle (2 Chronicles 20:17-26). When God's people trusted and praised Him He was able to bring victory. We have all learned what is meant by "a sacrifice of praise" (Hebrews 13:15).

4. *Give what you have.* "These commandments that I give you today are to be upon your hearts. Impress them on your children. Talk about them when you sit at home and when you walk along the road, when you lie down and when you get up" (Deuteronomy 6:6,7).

As my attitude began to change, so did my ability to be a mother. My children needed to see an example of one who truly trusted God in all things; one who was not afraid, but had hope for the future. I recognized the devastation they were experiencing and saw their inability to express how they felt. I started having family talks. I gave them the freedom to always express their feelings regardless of what they were, as long as they showed respect. I encouraged and modeled to them the importance of a daily devotional life. I prayed with them each day, telling them of God's promises to our family. We started having Communion twice a month. When we broke bread together, we brought our tithes and offerings to the Lord. We blessed what God had given us and asked Him to show himself strong on our behalf.

We started taking walks together and shared our hurts and aspirations. When I made a mistake, I told them I was sorry. I told them how I valued them and encouraged their opinions. I made sure they knew that "they were not divorced," neither had they played any part in what had happened. I watched what I did, realizing they would most likely follow my example.

The most important thing I did was to stay in God's Word, re-examining my life daily so I would have something worthwhile to give to my children. I couldn't give what I didn't have.

My children now know that God is their Father, and He is my husband (Psalm 68:5). They know that Jesus came to heal the brokenhearted (Isaiah 61:1-3). They have found strength from within that only God gives. Genesis 50:20 has been displayed in our lives. We truly understand what happens when God uses what was meant for evil for our good.

Ruth Hetzendorfer, Ed.D., is a counselor/associate professor at Southwestern Assemblies of God University in Waxahachie, Texas.

23
RESTORING BROKEN RELATIONSHIPS

By Richard D. Exley

The ultimate act of love and friendship is forgiveness. Without this selfless act, no family relationship can long survive intact.

Because we are fallen people in a fallen world, we sin against those we love. In turn, they sin against us. Sometimes we sin hastily in a moment of anger. Sometimes we sin thoughtlessly and do not consider the ramifications of our behavior. Sometimes we sin selfishly, deliberately, because we are thinking only of ourselves. And rarely do we sin cruelly, premeditatedly. Sin is part of our relationships; therefore, forgiveness must also be part.

Jesus understood the human heart and condition. Peter asked Him, " 'Lord, how many times shall I forgive my brother when he sins against me? Up to seven times?' "

"Jesus answered, 'I tell you, not seven times, but seventy-seven times' " (Matthew 18:21,22, NIV).

Why would Jesus make such a big thing out of forgiveness? Because sin is such a big thing in our relationships. And sin cannot be undone; it can only be forgiven.

Unforgiveness births bitterness, and bitterness is a luxury we cannot afford. It is not an isolated emotion directed toward one individual or situation; it's an infection which spreads throughout the human psyche. It distorts the personality, colors one's perception of events and other people, and even affects how one perceives God. It robs life of joy. Untreated, it will ravish an individual, leaving him just a shell of his former self.

Bitterness toward another may or may not hurt the person against whom it is directed, but it will destroy the soul of the one who harbors it.

One difficulty in dealing with unforgiveness is getting people to realize they need to forgive. A man spent an hour recounting a long list of past hurts. When I gently suggested he might need to deal with his bitterness, he became indignant and assured me he harbored no ill feelings. If you cannot talk about past hurts and betrayals without experiencing strong emotions, then you are still dealing with unforgiveness.

Another giveaway is how a person reacts to a given situation. A man once lambasted me in the foyer just before the church service. His emotional response was out of proportion to the significance of the slight. If you constantly overreact, you too may be harboring unforgiveness.

What can you do to get rid of it? The cure is not easy—forgiveness.

Feelings of forgiveness almost never precede the actual act. You must by an act of your will pronounce forgiveness; then you can expect the desired emotions. Forgiveness is a choice, a spiritual discipline, rather than a feeling. If you wait for the emotional motivation, you will spend much of your life in a self-made prison. Learn to act out your forgiveness, and you will discover a life of joy and freedom.

I have discovered three simple steps which facilitate forgiveness.

First, *confess your feelings.* Many Christians tend to deny their feelings when they are painful or if they seem unacceptable. But there can be no act of forgiveness until such feelings are acknowledged and the need to forgive faced up to.

Second, *acknowledge you are powerless to change what you feel, and then give God permission to change your feelings.* Ask Him to help you love with His love the person who hurt you.

Then release the offending party. Let go of every desire for revenge, every thought of getting even or making the other person pay.

Many are afraid that if they do not punish the offending party, no one will. They are afraid to give God permission to change their feelings because they fear He will do it, and they are not yet ready to take that step. But we cannot afford to wait until we are ready. Life is too short.

Third, *in prayer forgive each person who has injured you.* For example: "God, I forgive (name) for humiliating me." "Lord, I forgive (name) for lying about me." "Father, I forgive (name) for . . . ." You were not sinned against generally, but specifically, so you must forgive specifically.

These steps are not an instantaneous once-for-all cure-all, but a strategy for handling bitterness and practicing forgiveness. These steps like prayer open us to the resources of God.

Few things in life are more painful than a broken relationship. It is a universal pain, an inevitable consequence of our fallen condition.

Yet, there is nothing which can compare with the gift of forgiveness. To know the healing power it works on a broken heart is joy indeed. It restores that which was lost. It heals that which was wounded.

The miracle of forgiveness does not change the past. Nobody can undo the wrongs we have suffered, the pain we have inflicted. But it does redeem the present and unlock the future. When I forgive my friend his sin, I release him to know once again the blessedness of our relationship. When he forgives me, I experience new life. Forgiveness gives me a second chance. This time I will do better. I will share more deeply, trust more completely. Together we will drink deeply of the cup of forgiveness and love again.

Forgiveness will build a relationship that lasts.

Excerpted from *Life's Bottom Line*, by Richard D. Exley (Tulsa: Honor Books, 1990), with permission.

Richard D. Exley, an Assemblies of God minister and author, lives in Broken Arrow, Oklahoma.

For additional copies of *Family: How to have a healthy Christian home,* call:

Gospel Publishing House
1 (800) 641-4310
Please request product number 02HY1034.

To subscribe to the *Pentecostal Evangel* magazine, call 1 (800) 641-4310.